# Classic Fine Art Nudes Volume Two

By

Carl Scott Harker

## Table of Contents

Introduction .................................................................................. Page 4

Female Vampire by Albert Joseph Pénot ................................................. Page 5

After The Bath by Edgar Degas ............................................................ Page 6

Nude Woman Asleep in Office Chair by William Merritt Chase ........ Page 7

Nude Mermaid with Fancy Hair by George Barbier ......................... Page 8

Lovers on the Couch by George Barbier ............................................ Page 9

Witches Going To Their Sabbath by Luis Ricardo Falero ................. Page 10

The Birth of the Milky Way by Peter Paul Rubens .............................. Page 11

Nude Woman With Long Hair by Edvard Munch .............................. Page 12

Nude Woman On a Couch by Kenyon Cox ....................................... Page 13

Water Nymph by Gaston Brussiere ..................................................... Page 14

Female Nude Drawing by Gustav Klimt ............................................. Page 15

Japanese Nude Woman Applying Make-up by Ito Shinsui ............... Page 16

Nude Woman Holding a Black Cat by Capelari Fritz ......................... Page 17

Nude Self-Portrait with Palette by Richard Gersti ............................... Page 18

Poedooa, the Daughter of Oree by John Webber .............................. Page 19

The Choice Between the Young and Old by Cornelis Van Haarlem ........
........................................................................................................ Page 20

Nude Woman by Giorgio De Chirico ................................................... Page 21

College Refreshment by Thomas Rowlandson ................................... Page 22

The Dream by Henri Rousseau ........................................................... Page 23

Sorrow by Vincent Van Gogh ............................................................... Page 24

Cupid and Psyche in the Nuptial Bower by Hugh Douglas Hamilton ......
........................................................................................................ Page 25

Nude Playing With Cat by Ishikawa ................................................... Page 26

Tannhäuser at the Mountain of Venus by John Collie ....................... Page 27

Summer Nude by Frederick Carl Frieseke ........................................ Page 28

Nude in Pond by Warwick Goible .................................................. Page 29
Working in Marble by Jean-Léon Gérôme ........................................ Page 30
The Butterfly by Childe Hassam ..................................................... Page 31
The Birth of Venus by William Adolphe Bouguereau ...................... Page 32
Le Kimono Japonais by Delphin Enjolras ....................................... Page 33
Cupid & Psyche by William Adolphe Bouguereau .......................... Page 34
Venus Verticordia by Dante Gabriel Rossetti ................................. Page 35
Chinese Nude at Bath by Qui Ying ................................................. Page 36
Eve in the Garden by Paul Ranson ................................................. Page 37
Adam and Eve by Albrecht Durer ................................................... Page 38
Nude Bather by Pierre Auguste Renoir .......................................... Page 39
The Large Bathers by Pierre Auguste Renoir ................................. Page 40
She Goes Down to the Fresh Water by Paul Gauguin ..................... Page 41
Nude with a Hat by Vladimir Baranov Rossine ................................ Page 42
Nude Sitting by Théo Van Rysselberghe ........................................ Page 43
Reclining Nude by Tsugouharu Foujita .......................................... Page 44
Nude in Sunlit Wood by Childe Hassam ......................................... Page 45
Woman Lying Down Semi-Nude by Egon Schiele ........................... Page 46
Dancing Beauty by Hans Zatzka .................................................... Page 47
The Odalisque by Mariano Fortuny ................................................ Page 48
Study for Female Nude by Nakamura Tsune .................................. Page 49
Oriental Nude by Hans Hassenteufel ............................................. Page 50
Without Ceres and Bacchus, Venus Would Freeze by Hendrick Goltzius ...
.................................................................................................... Page 51
Nude From Behind by Paul Gauguin............................................... Page 52
Nude Young Woman Dressing by CW Eckersberg.......................... Page 53
Sitting Nude With Pillow by August Macke..................................... Page 54
About the Author .......................................................................... Page 55
Other Books by the Author ............................................................ Page 55
Copyright Notice ........................................................................... Page 56

## Introduction

Here is my second volume of classic fine art nudes for your enjoyment. In this book, you will again find a mixture of styles by artists from different time periods.

While there are different goddesses and Adam & Eve, here, many of the nude figures you will find in this volume are more of an expression of the artist's own style of painting, than just an excuse to show nudes in artwork that otherwise would be prohibited.

There is no doubt that the artists' presentations still celebrate the naked human form, but many paintings go beyond the presentation of the "ideal" nude figure to more realistic presentations or more abstract presentations.

Such variations are endless and reflect the state of art, the mind of the artist and especially the time when the artist lived. Thankfully, this art was preserved for our viewing pleasure, today, and to provide insights into the cultures of our past.

This book provides a selection of classic artistic nudes before the Internet, talking movies, graphic novels and TV were a part of our culture. And while cameras were beginning to take over the presentations of "actual reality," there were no cameras on every corner or iPhones in every pocket when this art was created.

Some of the artists in this book will be familiar to you, but I suspect you will also find artists unknown to you until now. Familiar or unfamiliar, this book holds a treasure of pleasant surprises of artistic discovery. Enjoy!

## Female Vampire by Albert Joseph Pénot

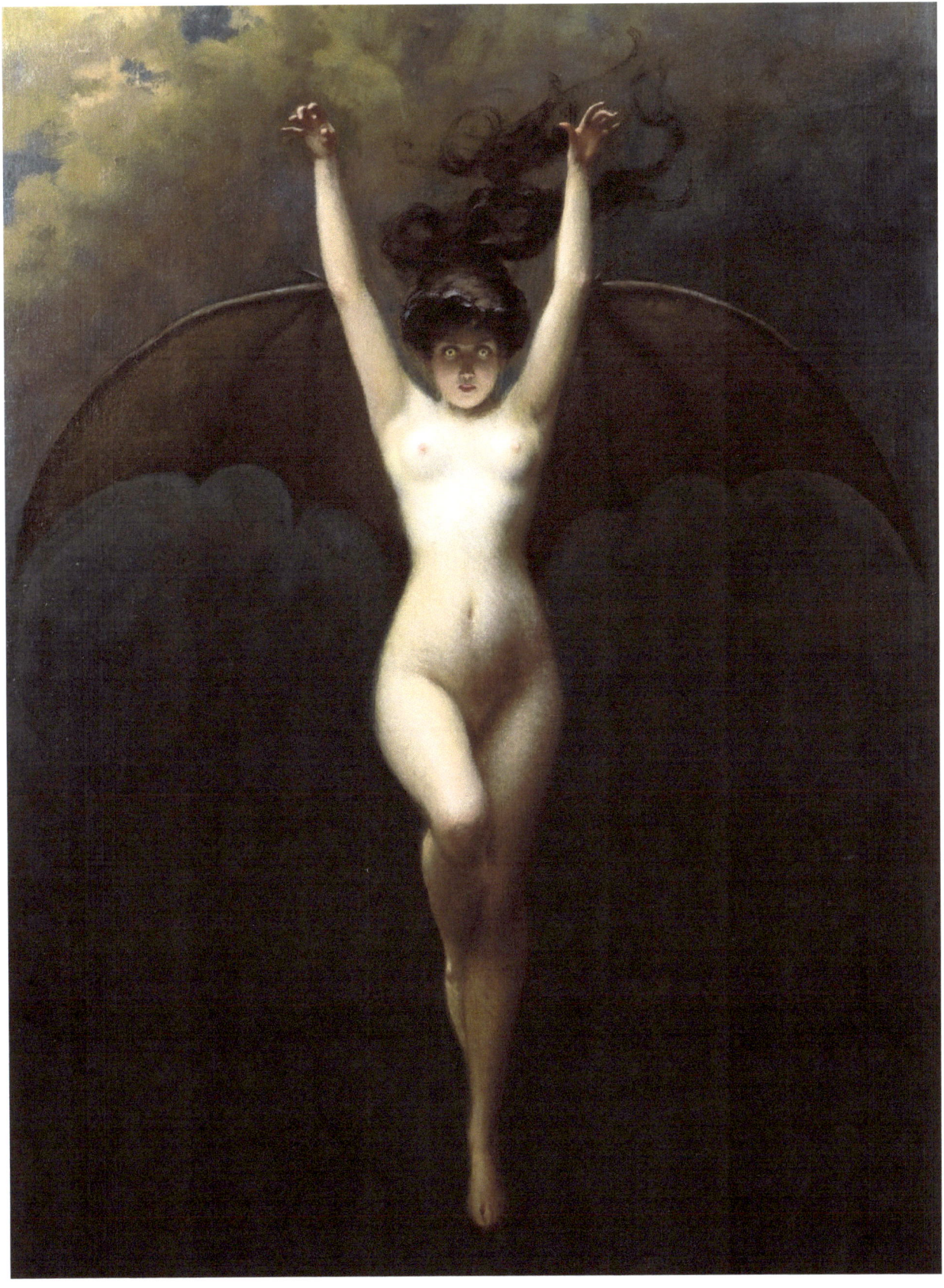

## After The Bath by Edgar Degas

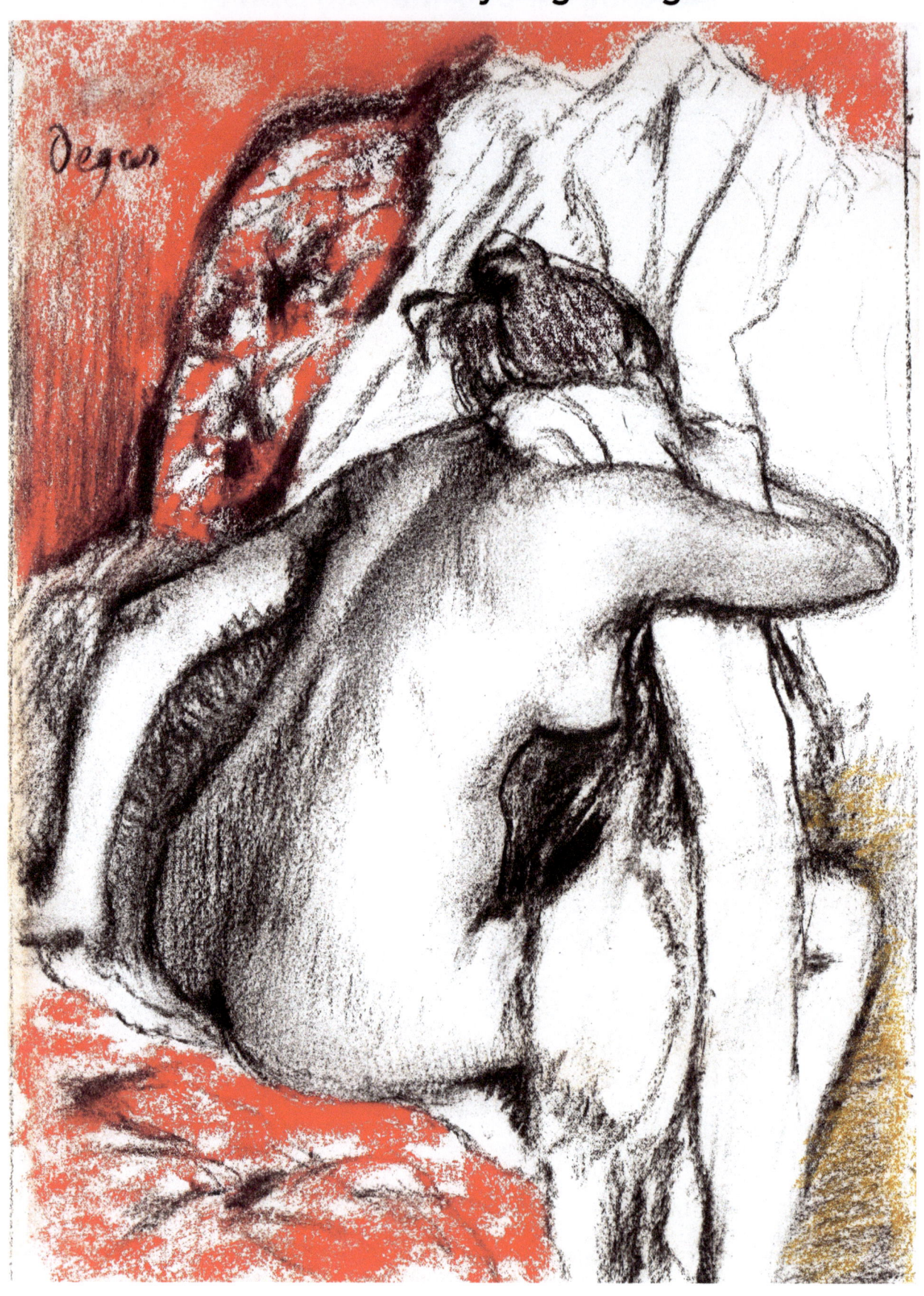

## Nude Woman Asleep in Office Chair by William Merritt Chase

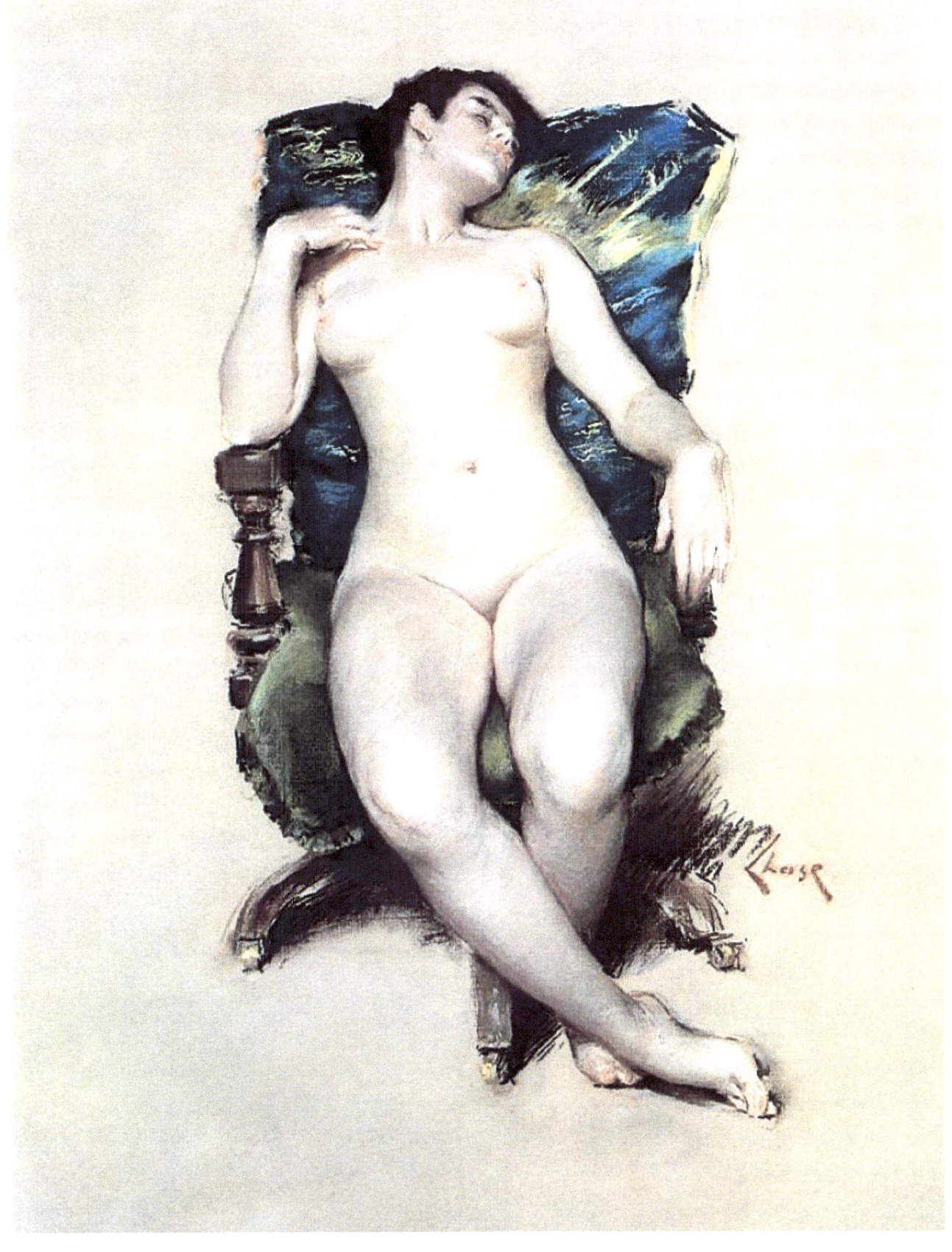

## Nude Mermaid with Fancy Hair by George Barbier

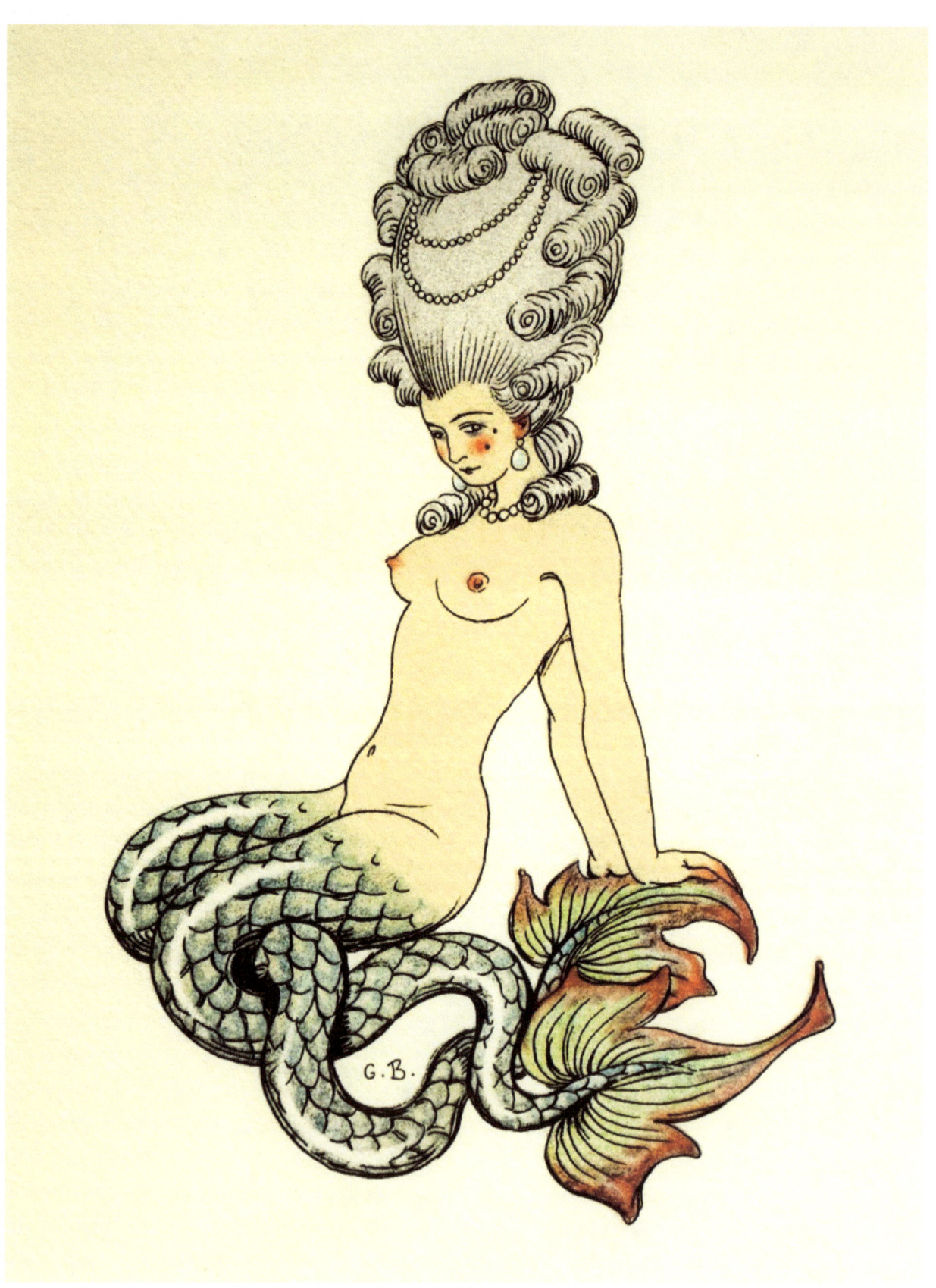

## Lovers on the Couch by George Barbier

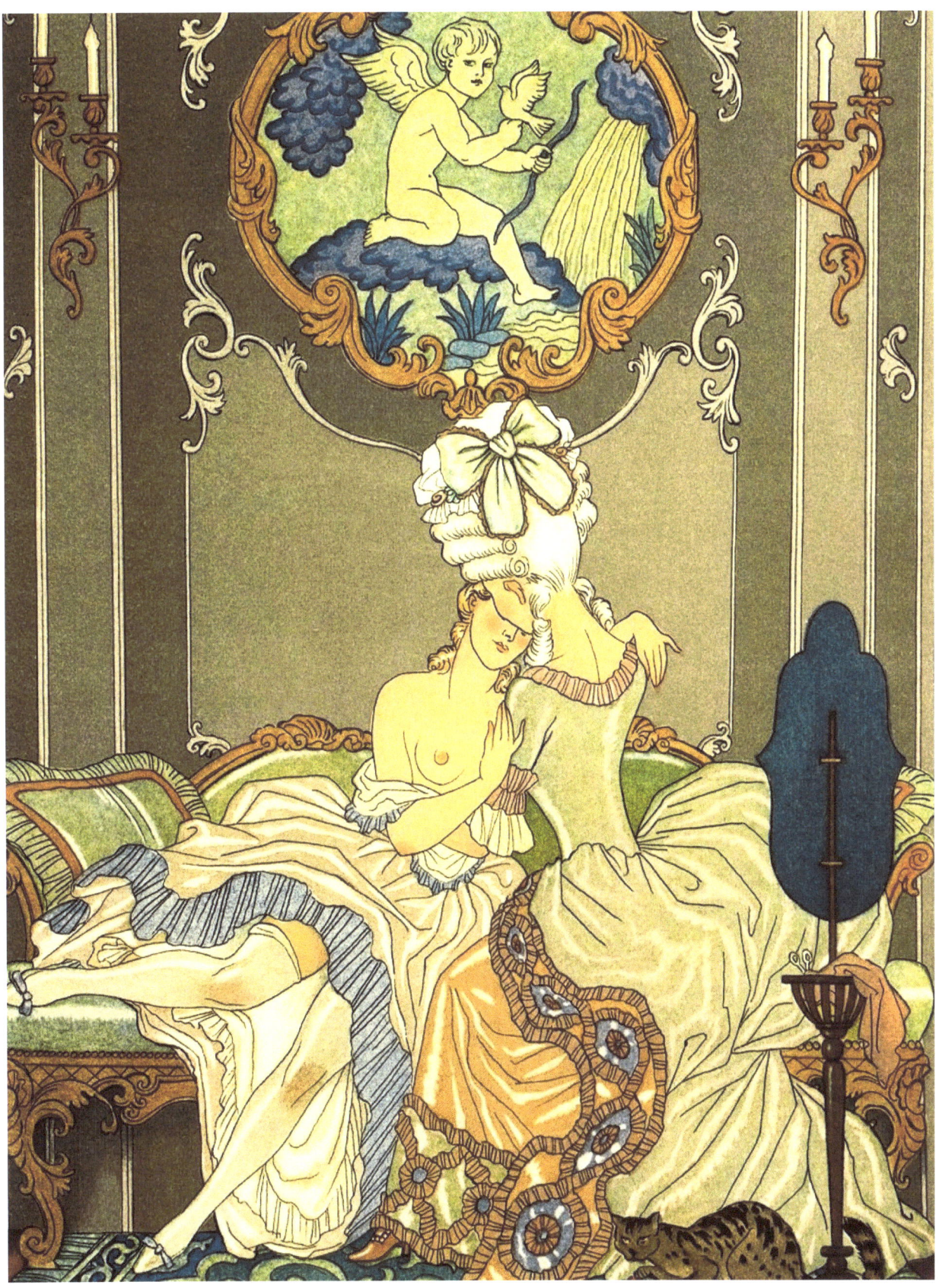

## Witches Going To Their Sabbath by Luis Ricardo Falero

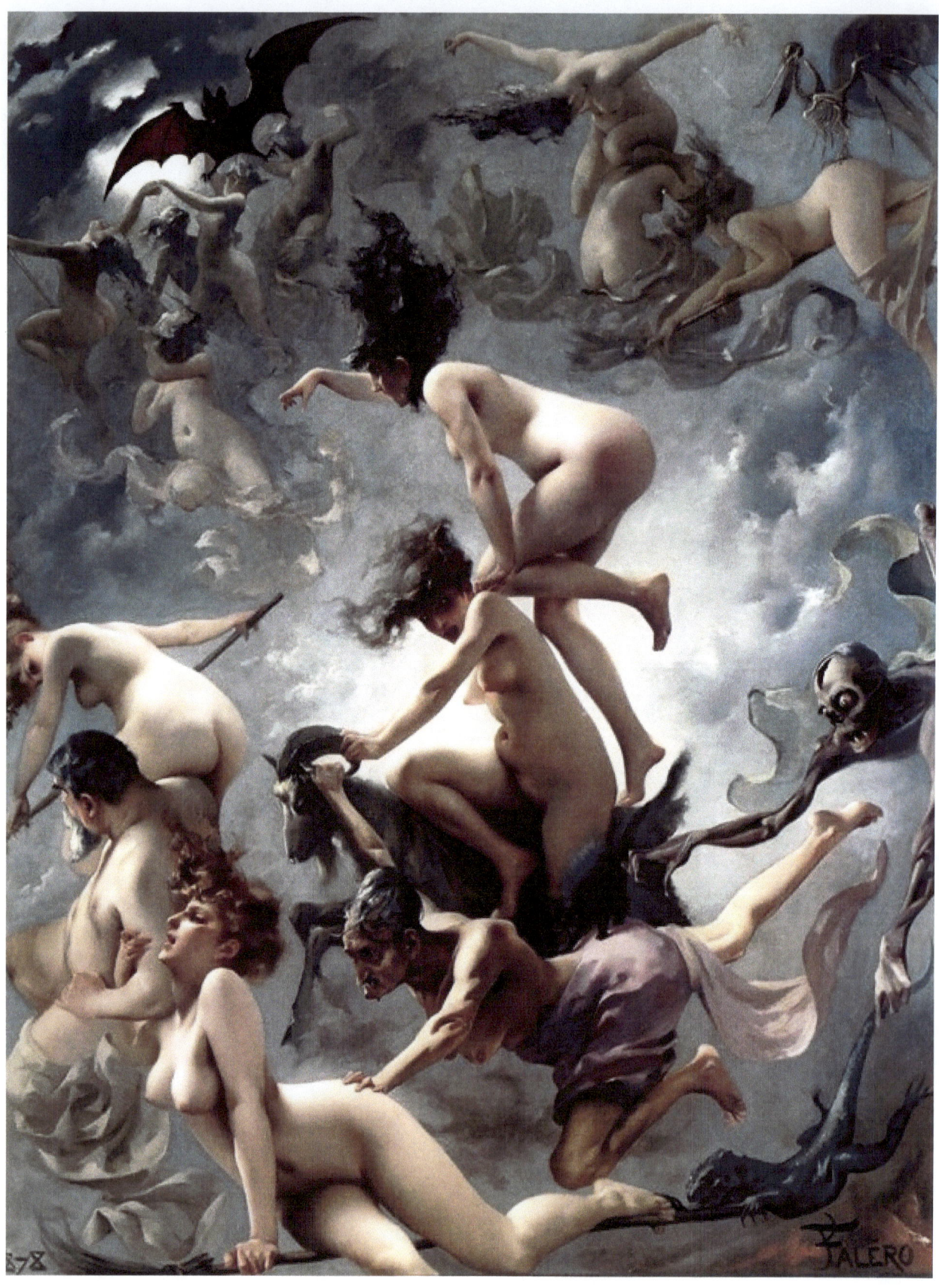

# The Birth of the Milky Way by Peter Paul Rubens

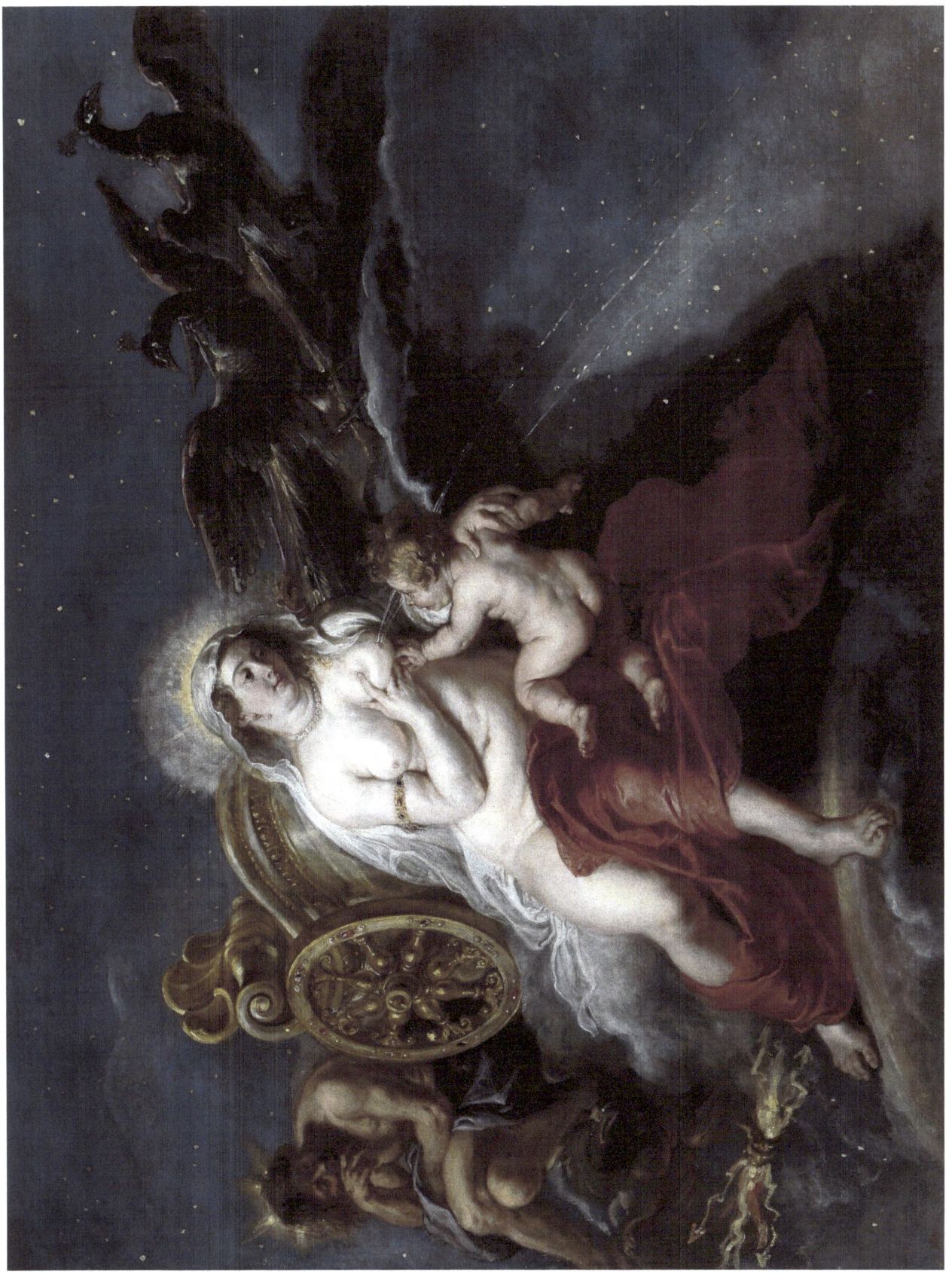

## Nude Woman With Long Hair by Edvard Munch

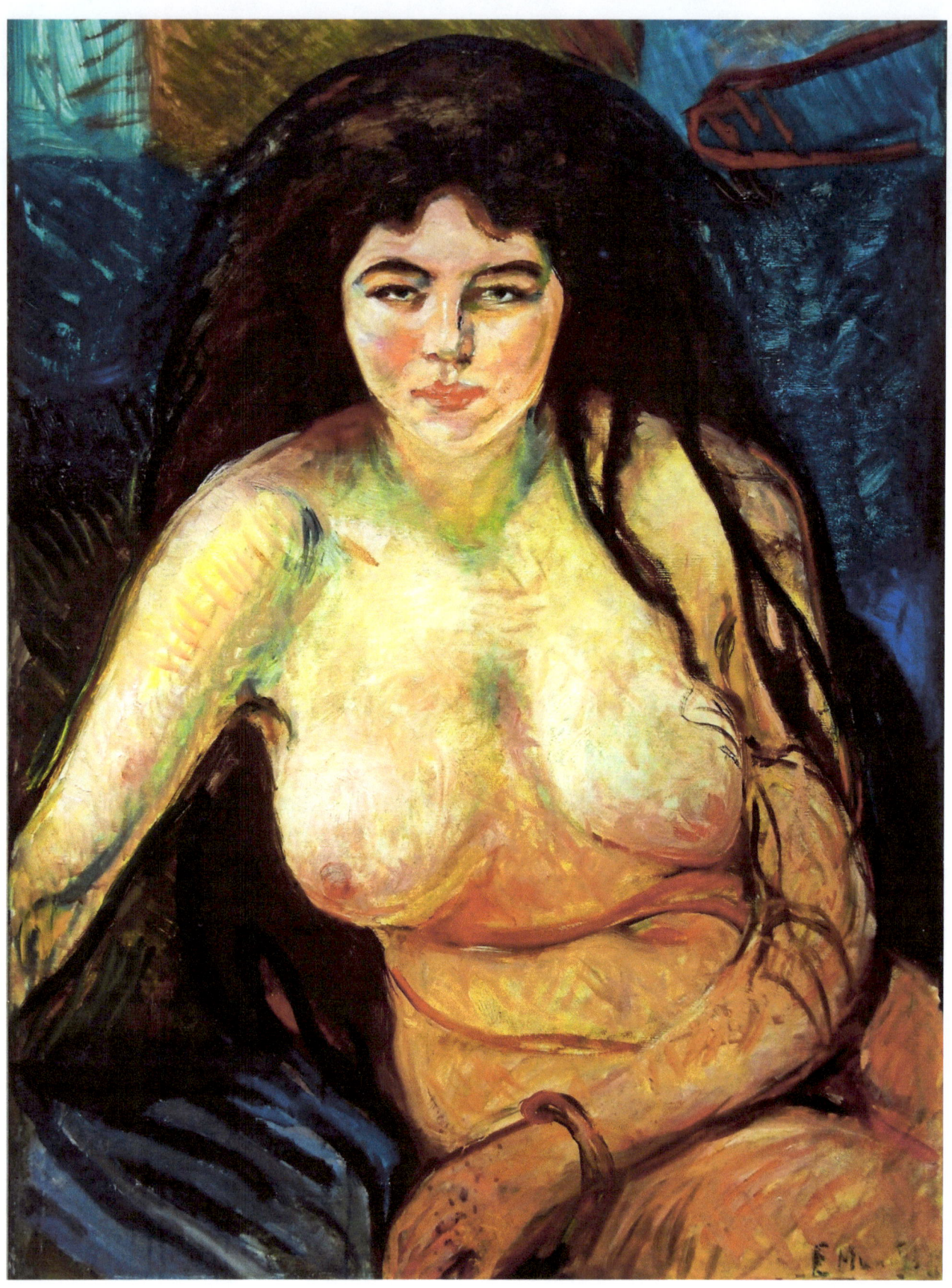

# Nude Woman On a Couch by Kenyon Cox

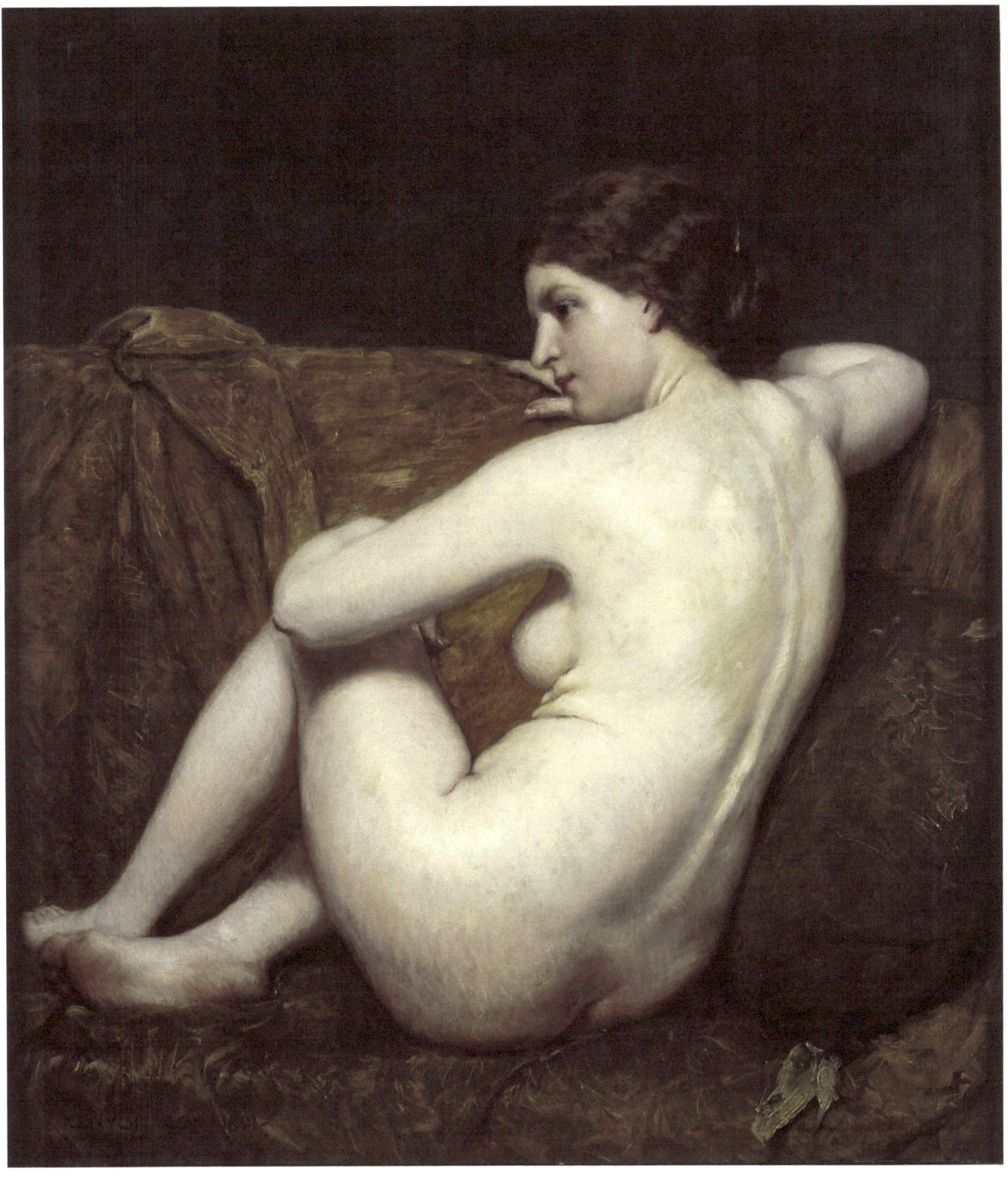

# Water Nymph by Gaston Brussiere

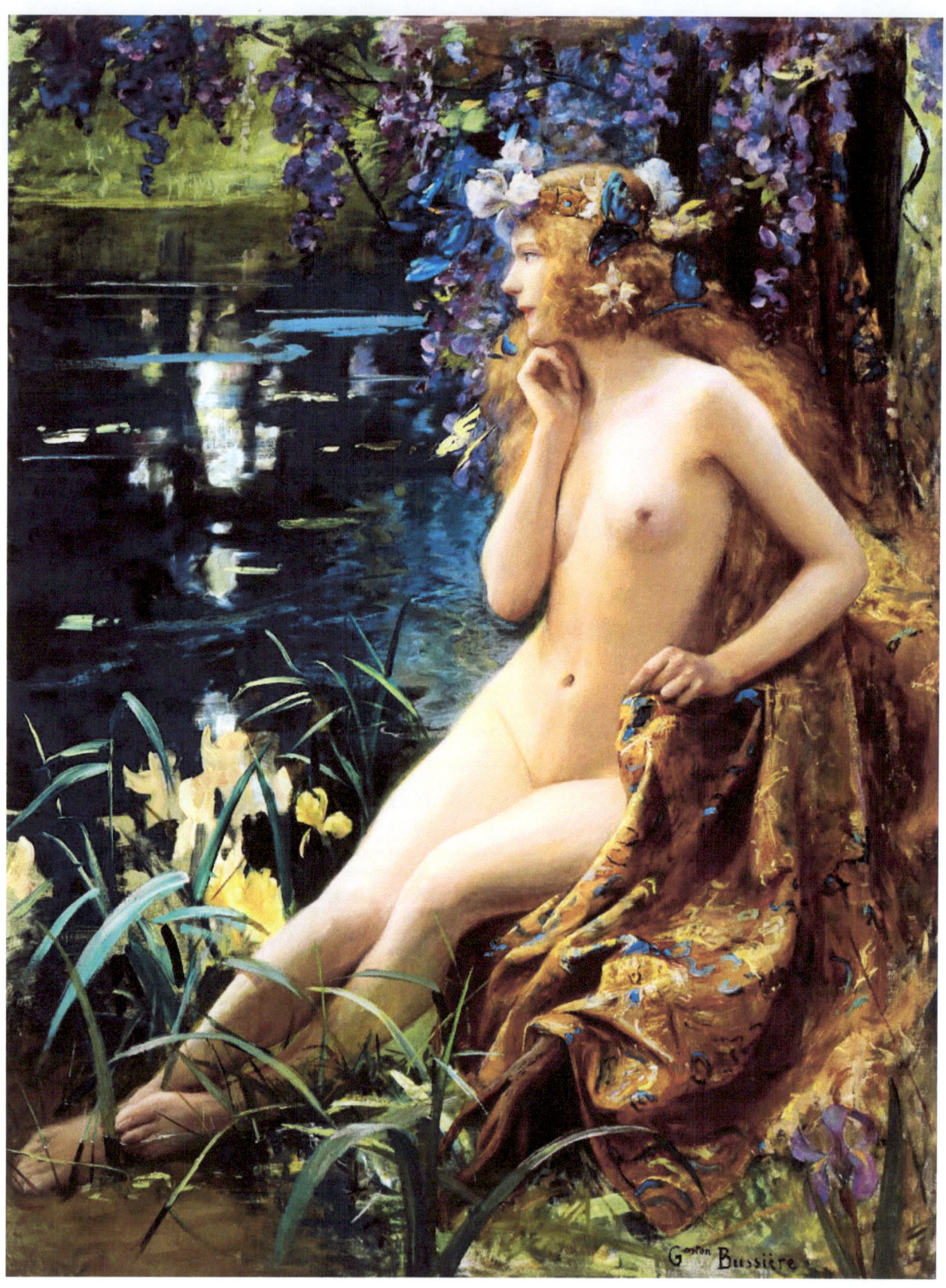

## Female Nude Drawing by Gustav Klimt

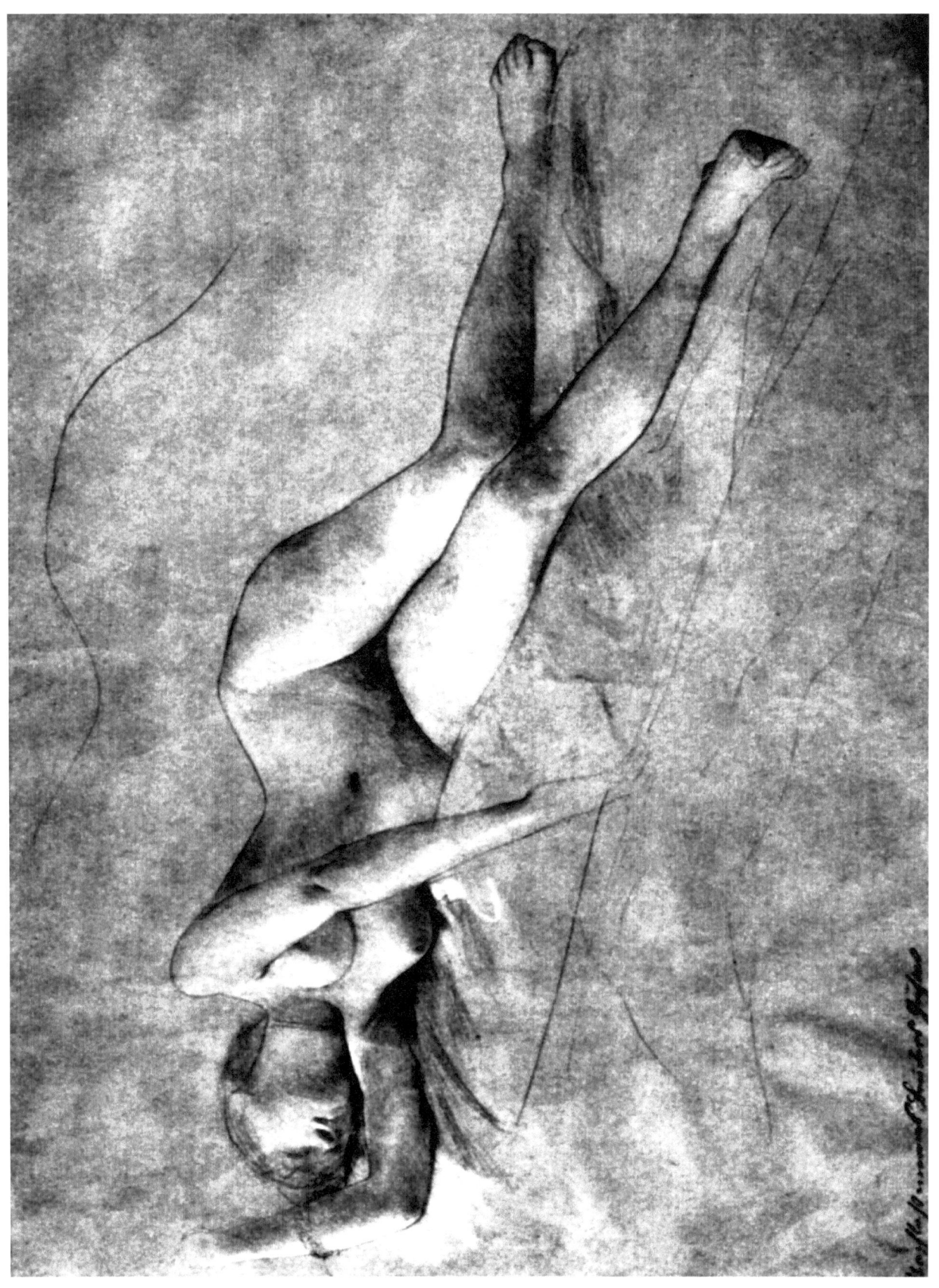

# Japanese Nude Woman Applying Make-up by Ito Shinsui

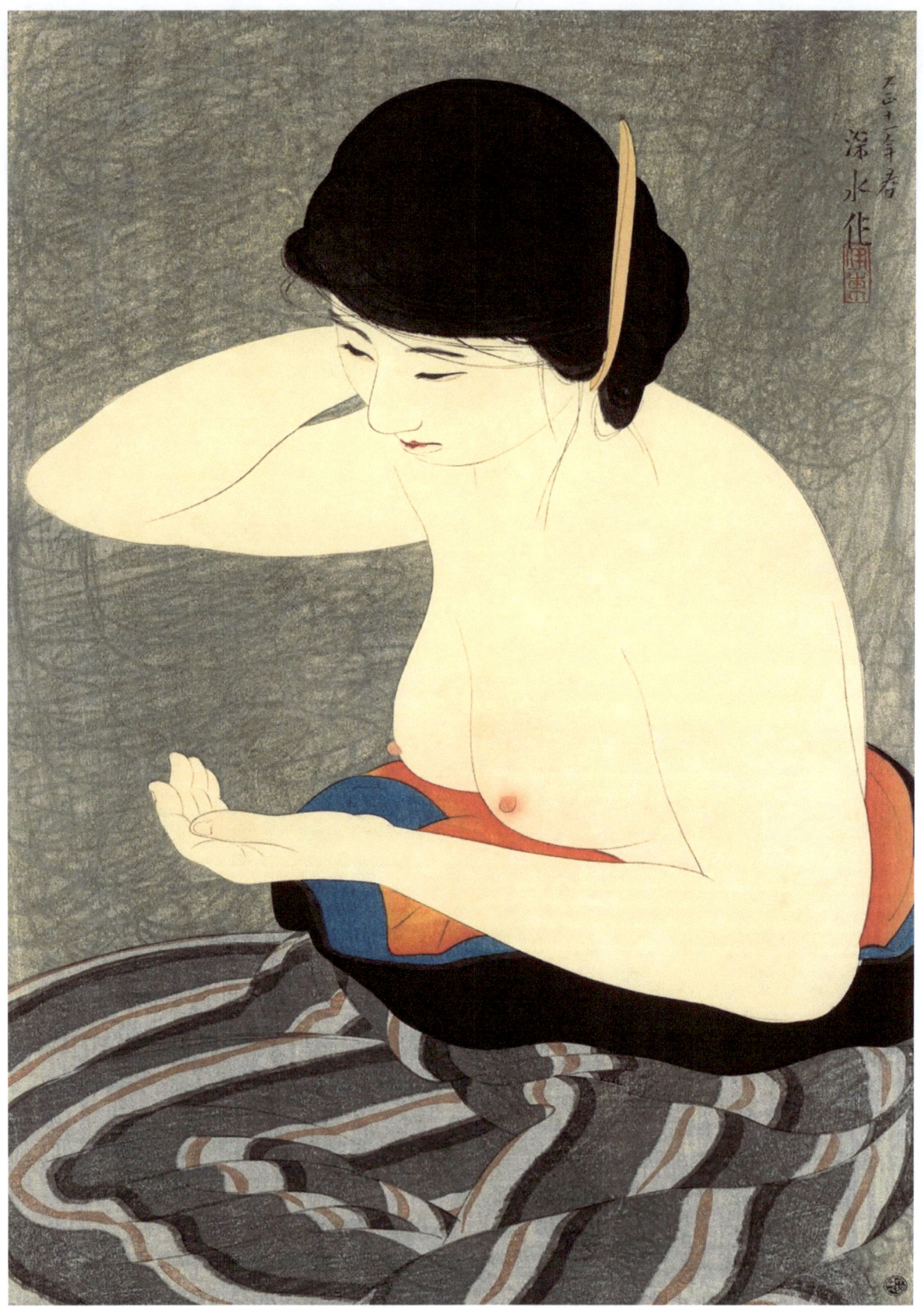

# Nude Woman Holding a Black Cat by Capelari Fritz

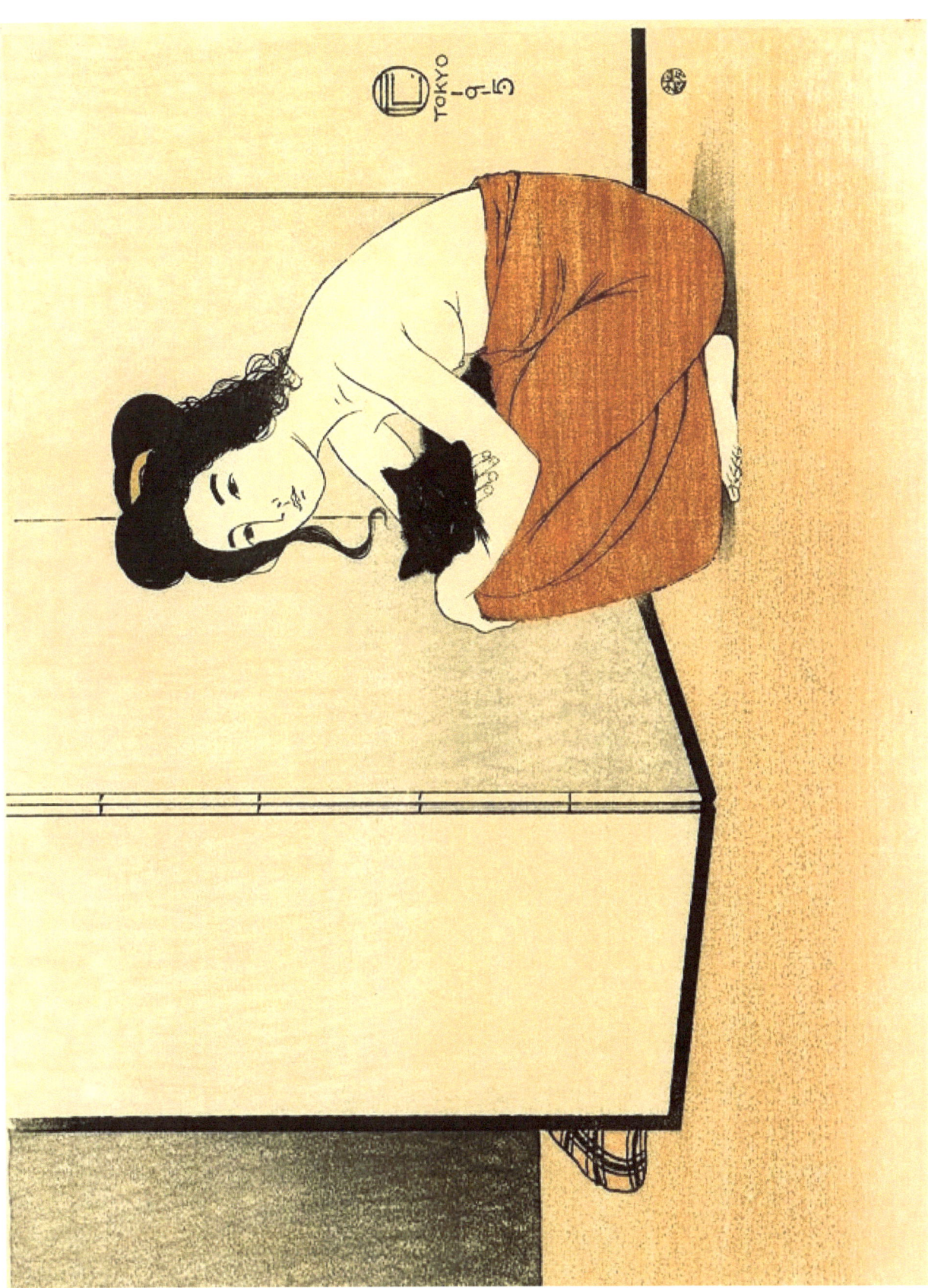

# Nude Self-Portrait with Palette by Richard Gersti

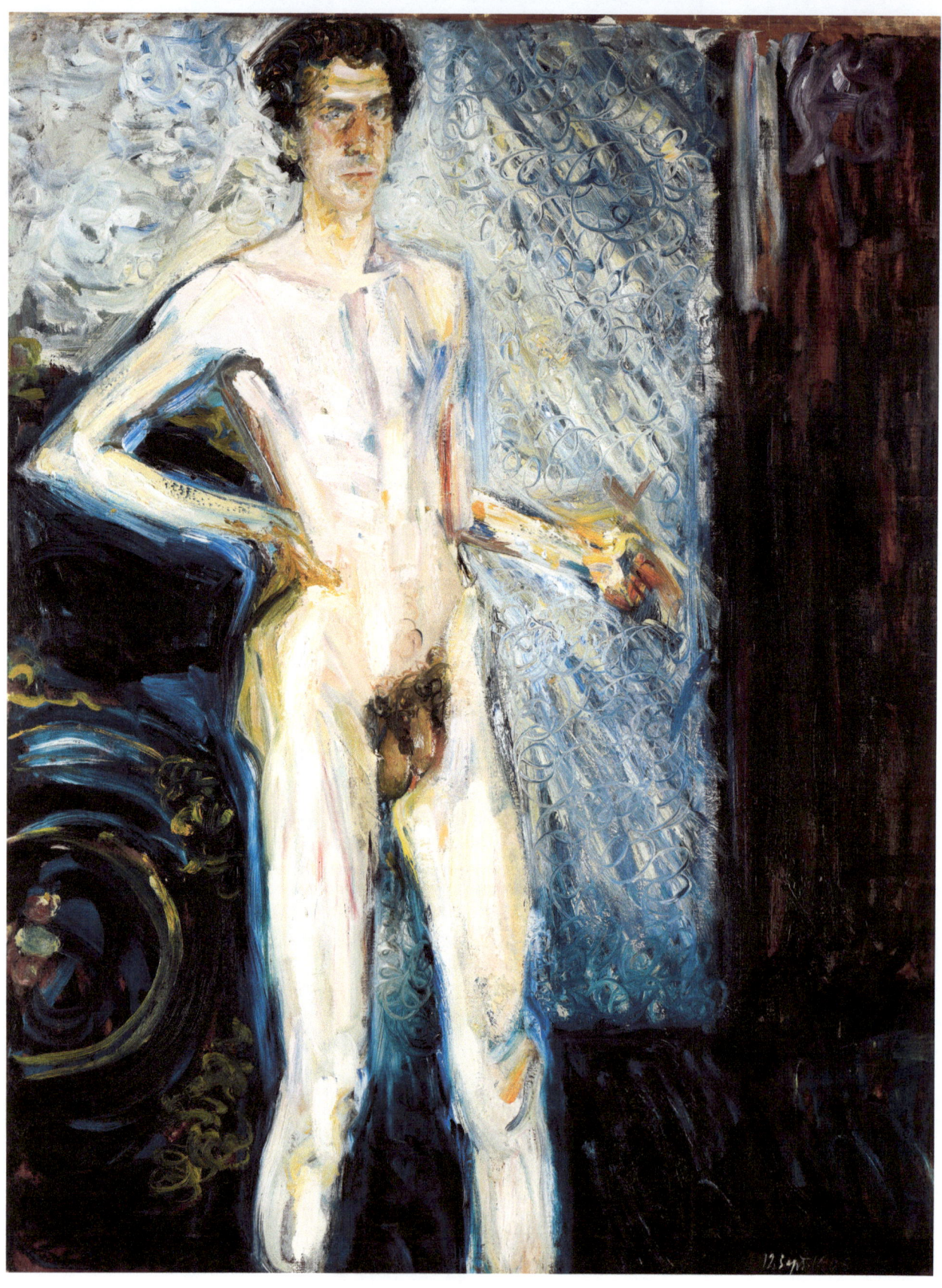

# Poedooa, the Daughter of Oree by John Webber

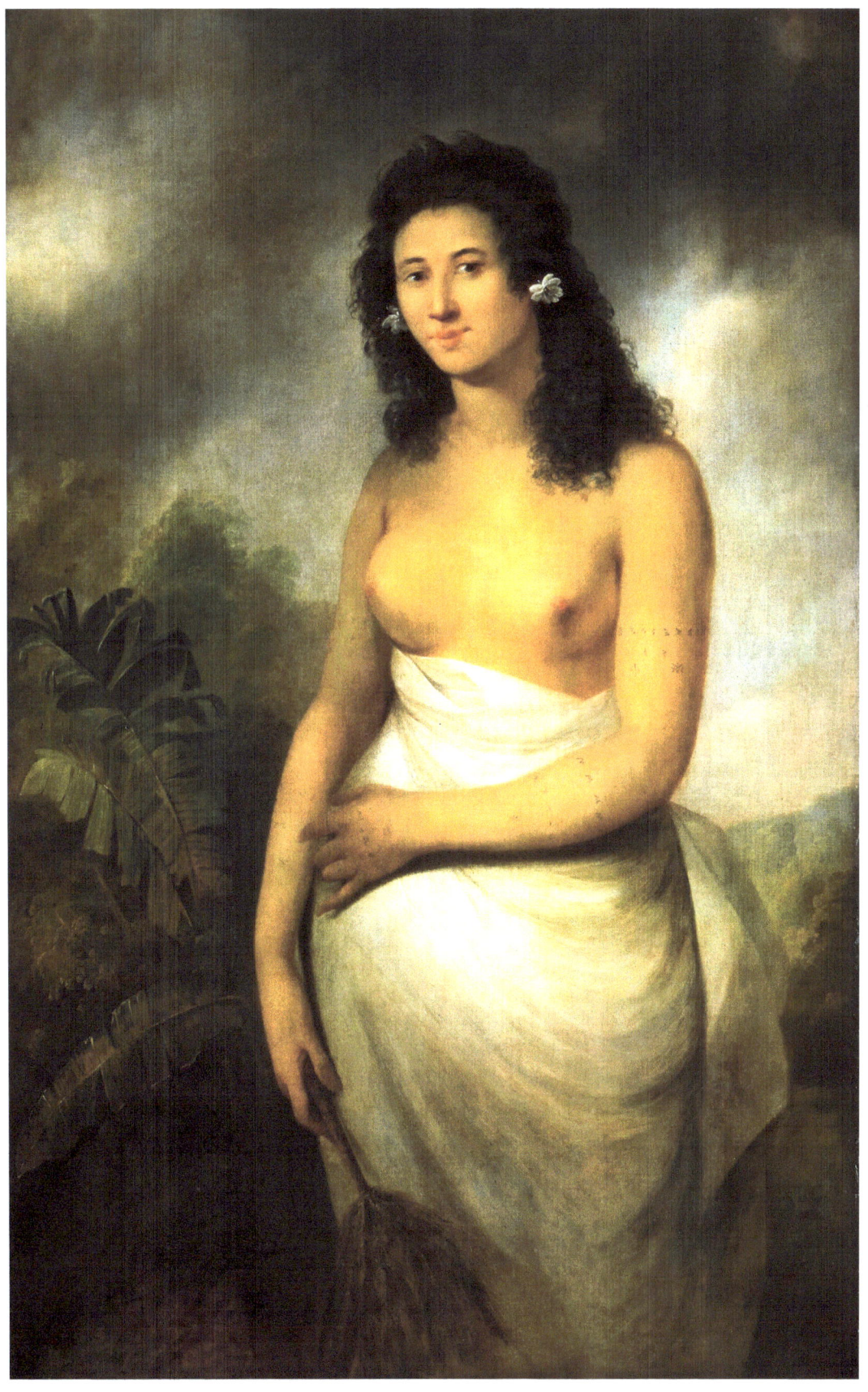

## The Choice Between the Young and Old by Cornelis Van Haarlem

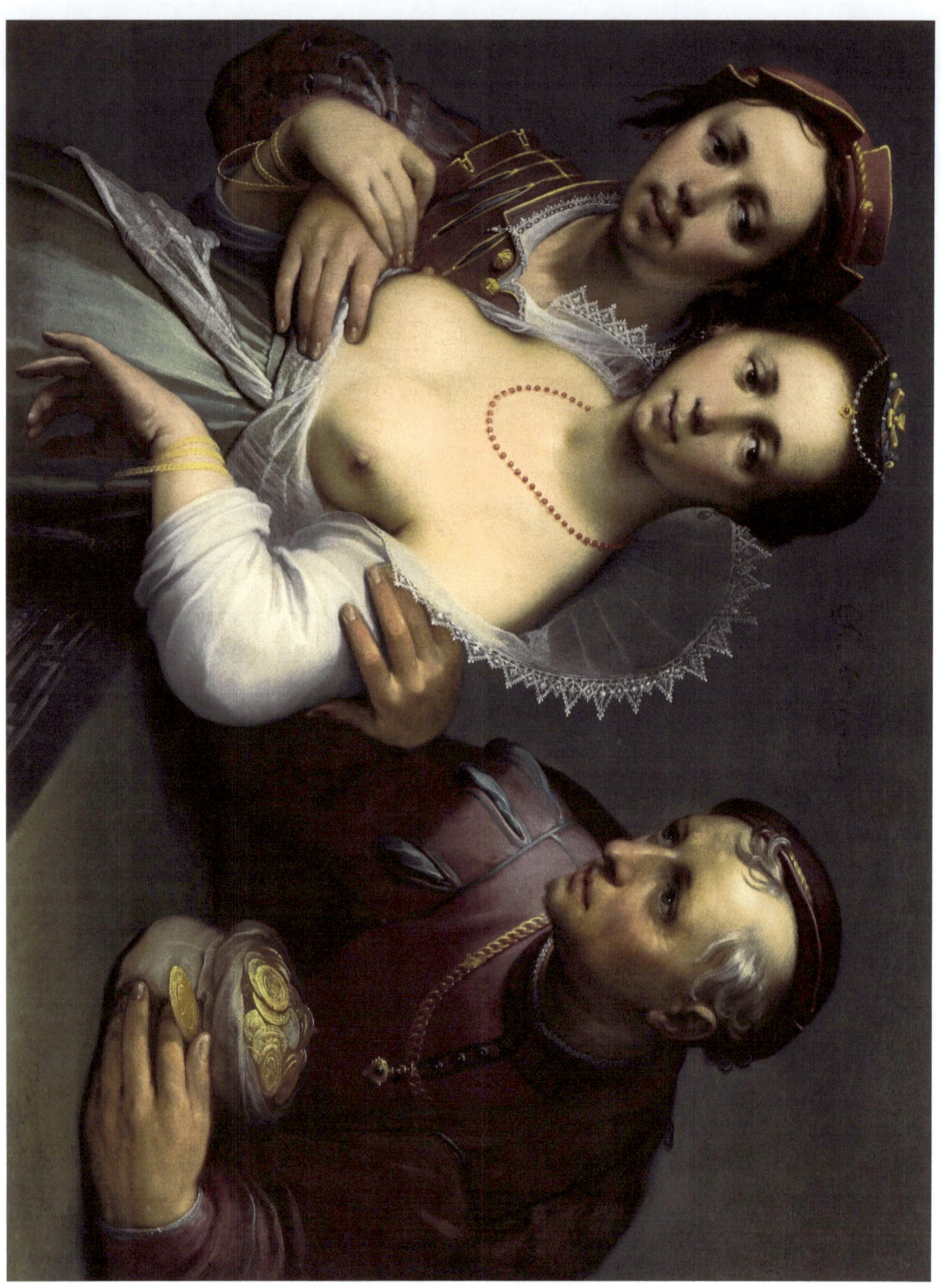

## Nude Woman by Giorgio De Chirico

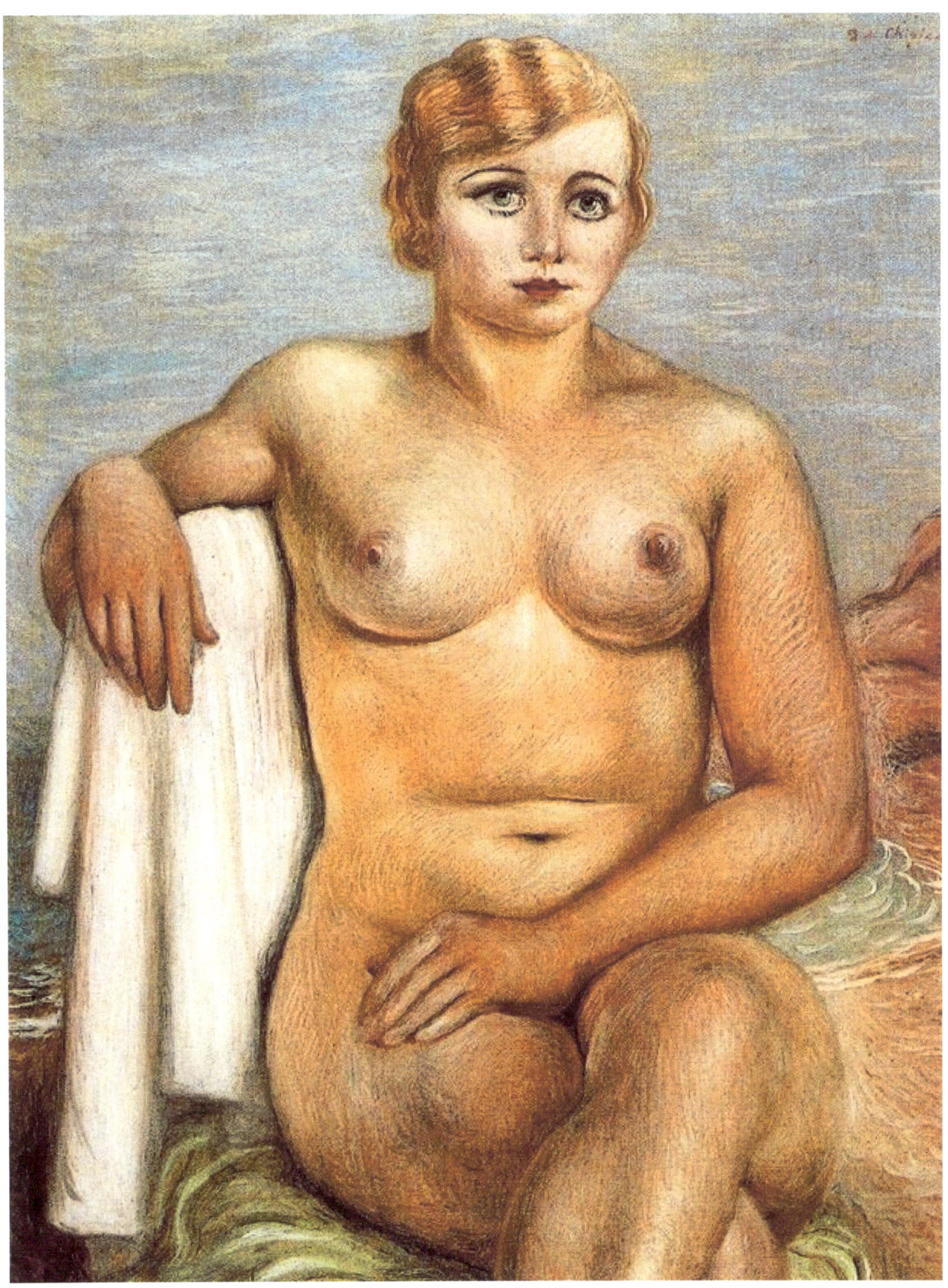

## College Refreshment by Thomas Rowlandson

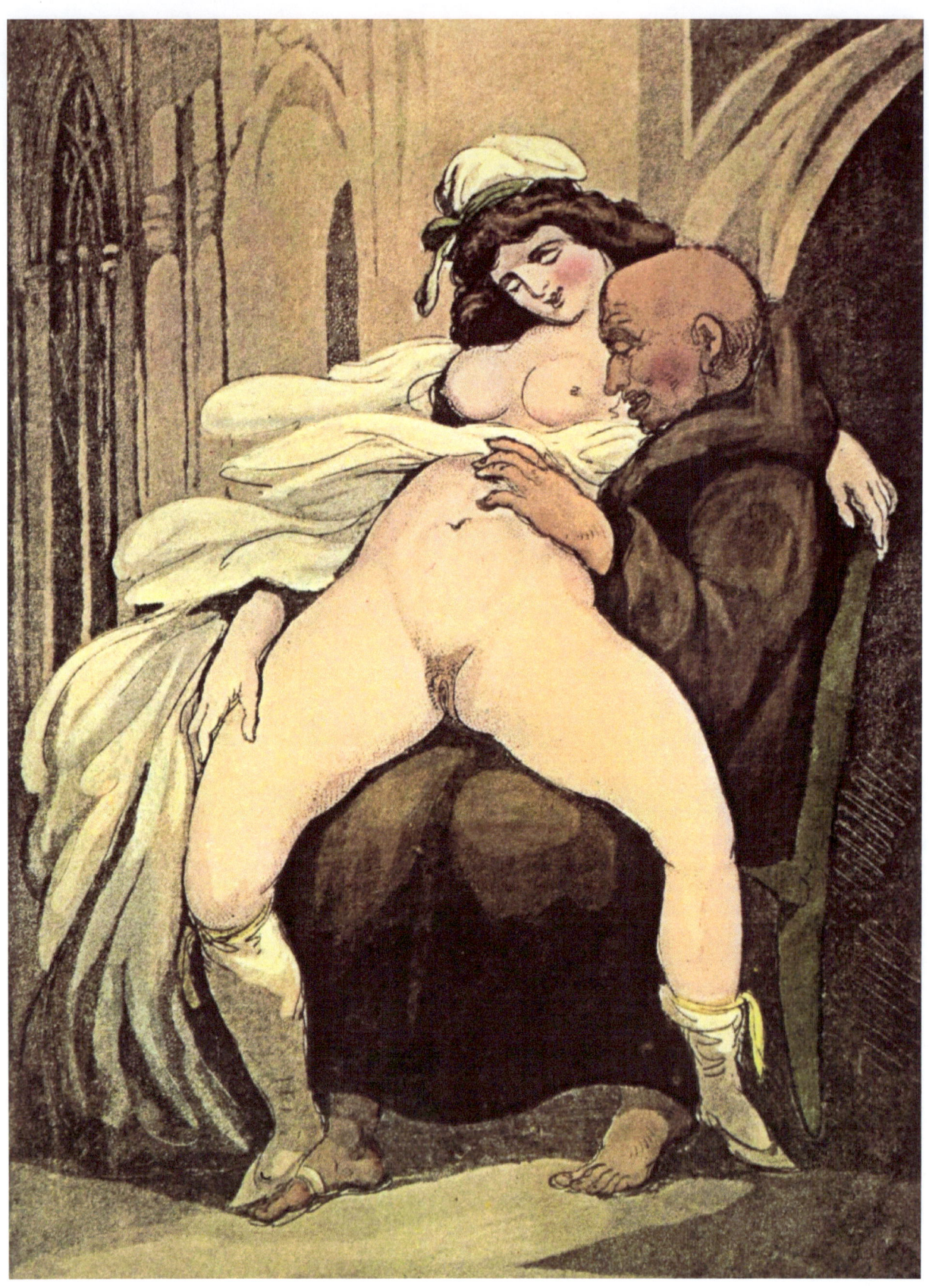

# The Dream by Henri Rousseau

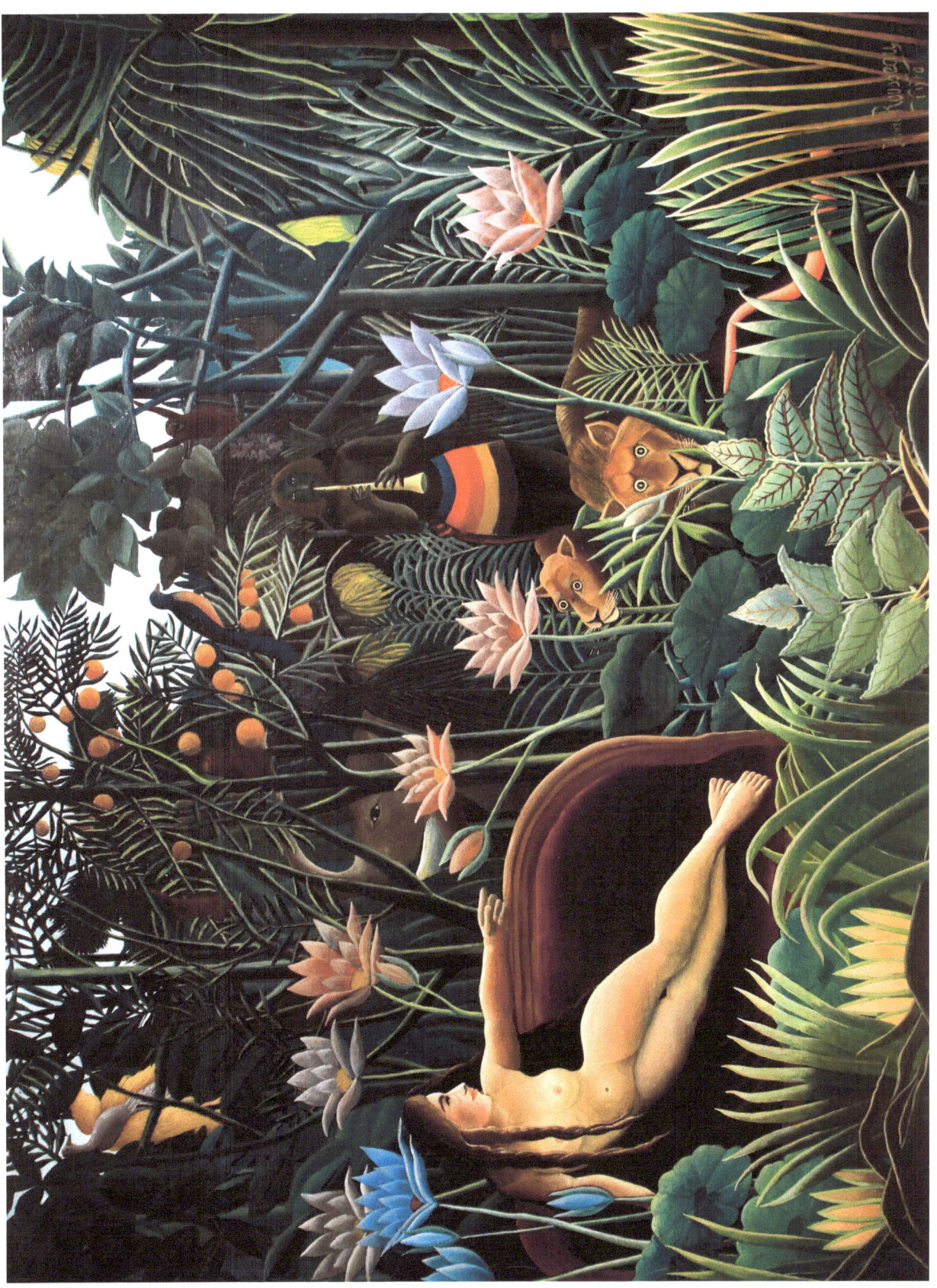

## Sorrow by Vincent Van Gogh

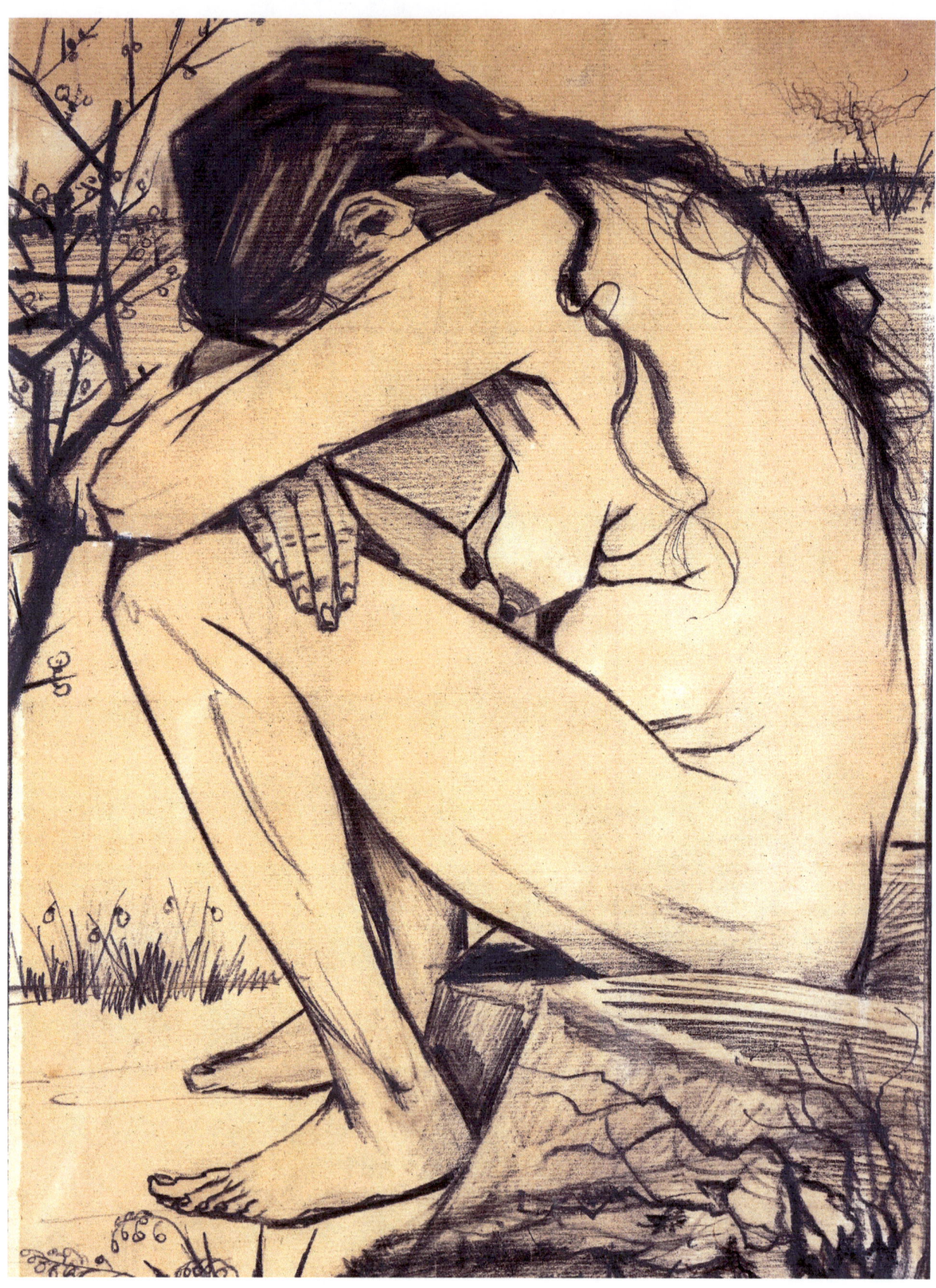

## Cupid and Psyche in the Nuptial Bower
## by Hugh Douglas Hamilton

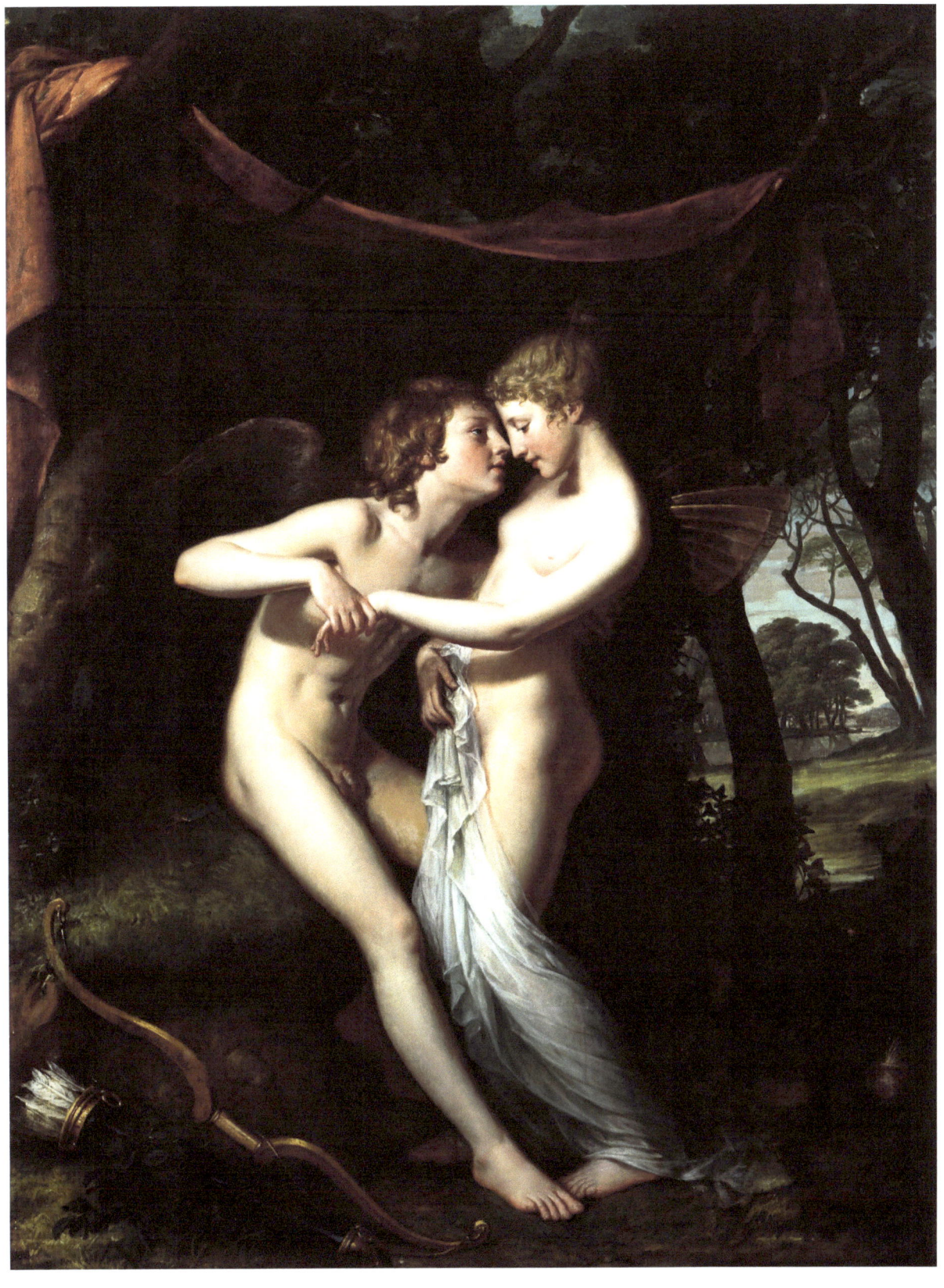

## Nude Playing With Cat by Ishikawa

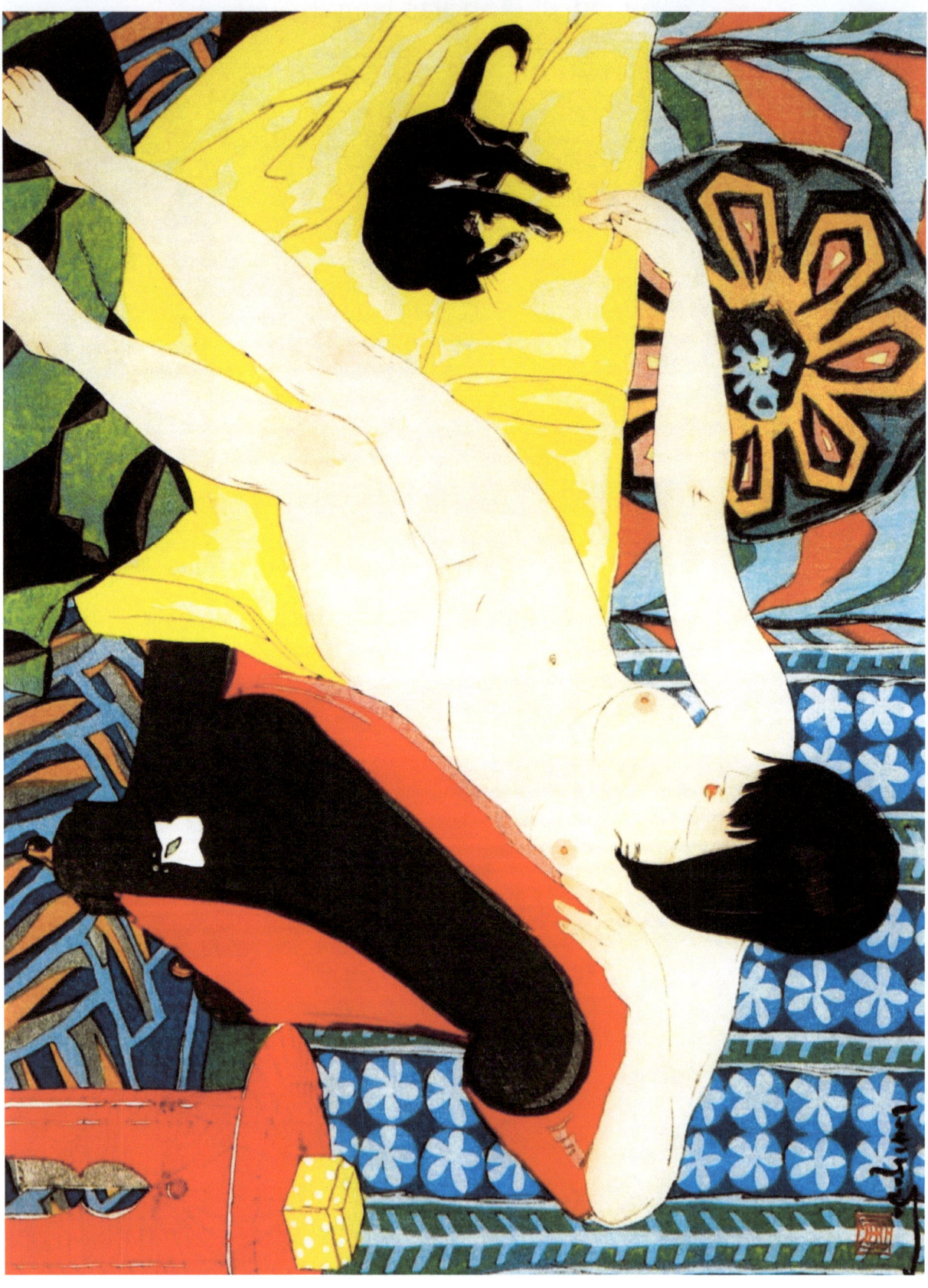

# Tannhäuser at the Mountain of Venus by John Collier

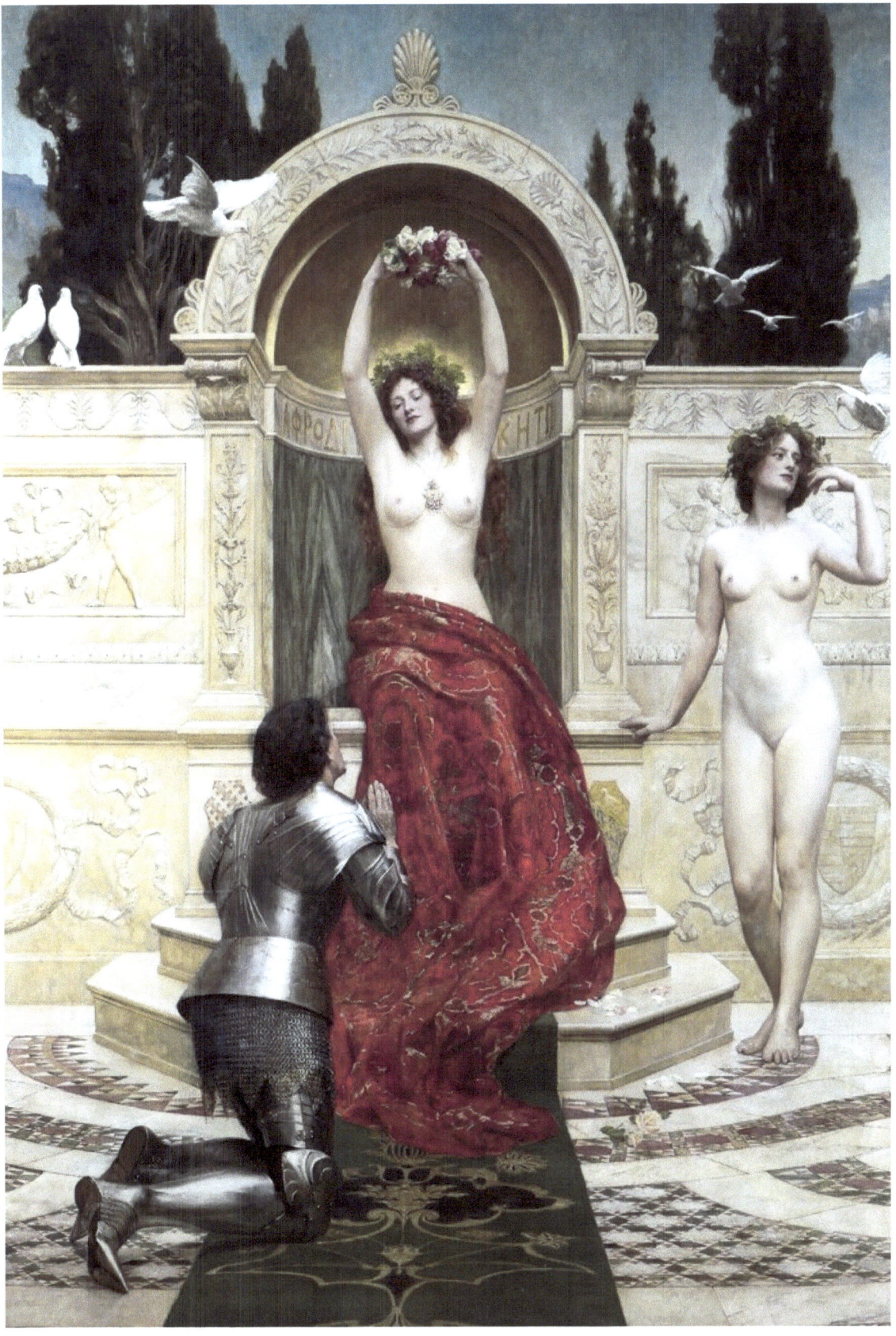

## Summer Nude by Frederick Carl Frieseke

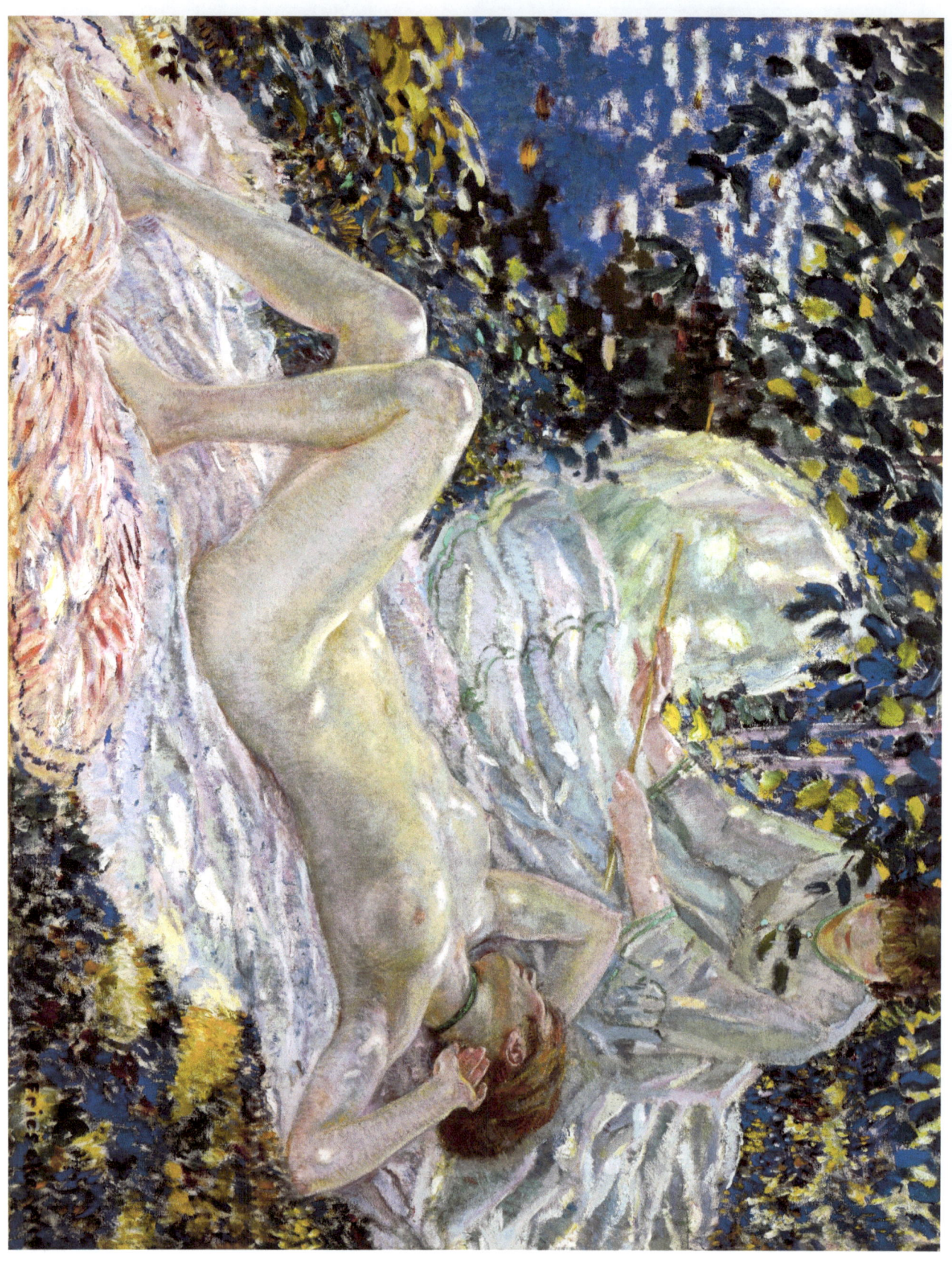

## Nude in Pond by Warwick Goible

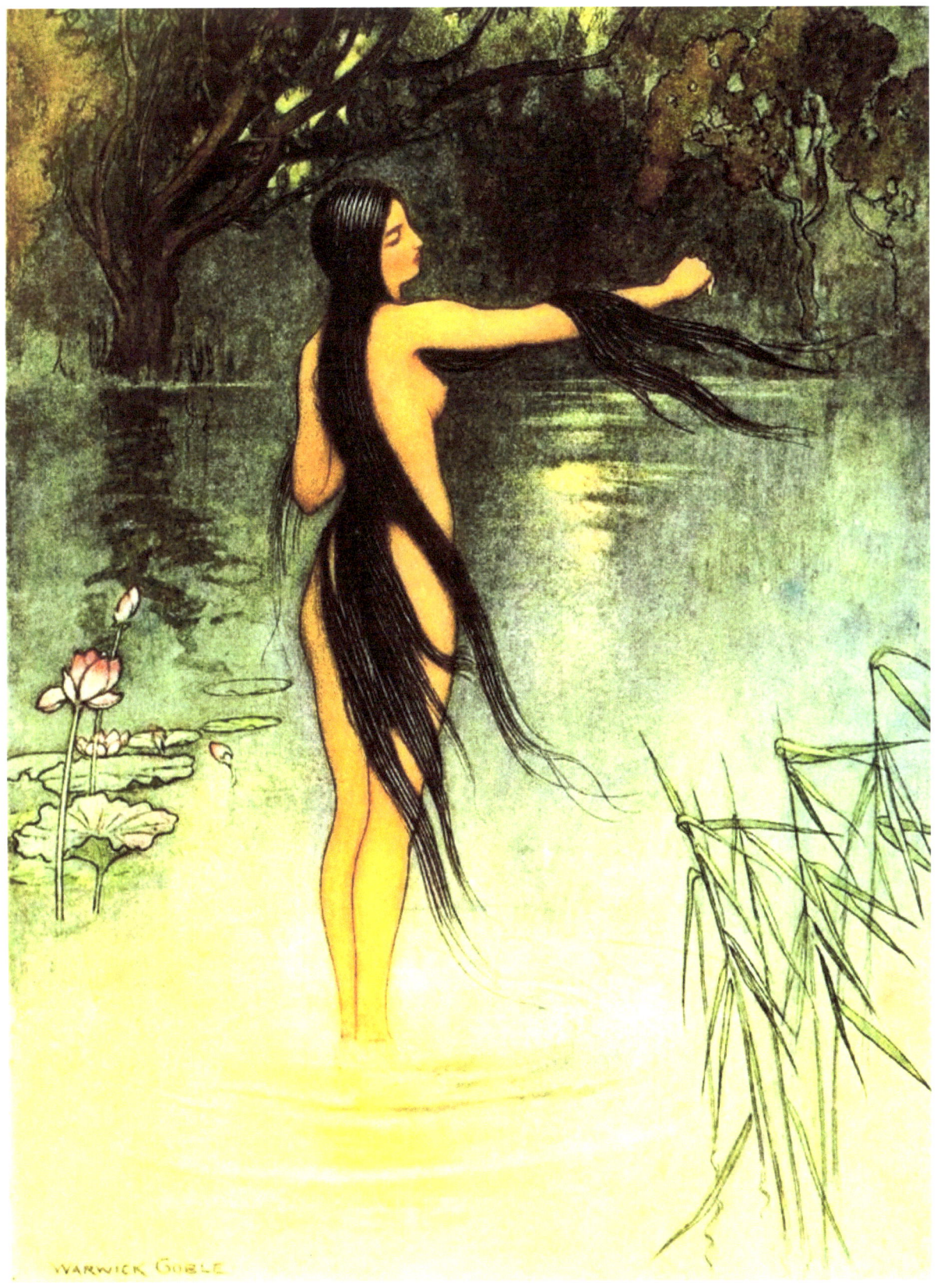

# Working in Marble by Jean-Léon Gérôme

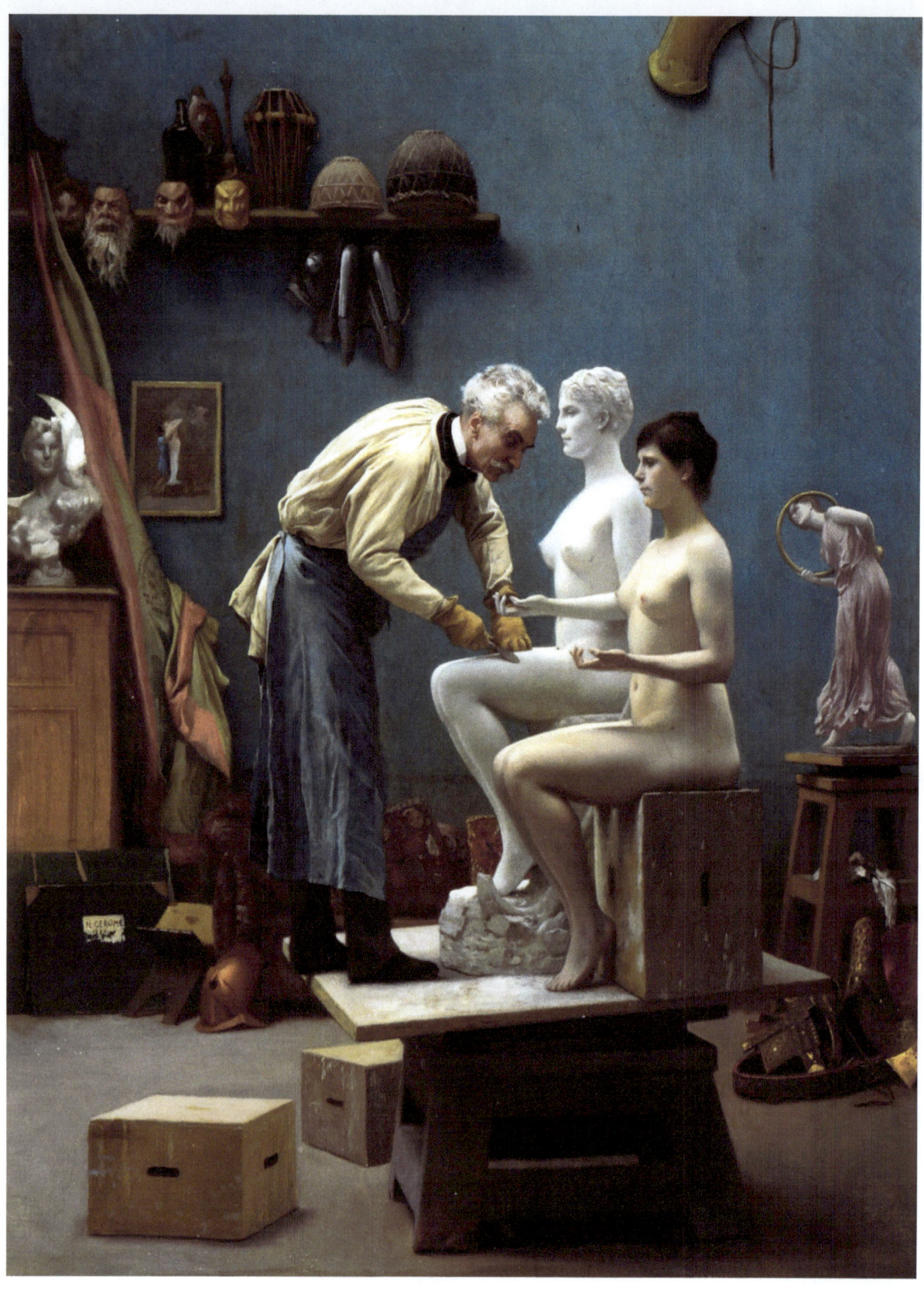

## The Butterfly by Childe Hassam

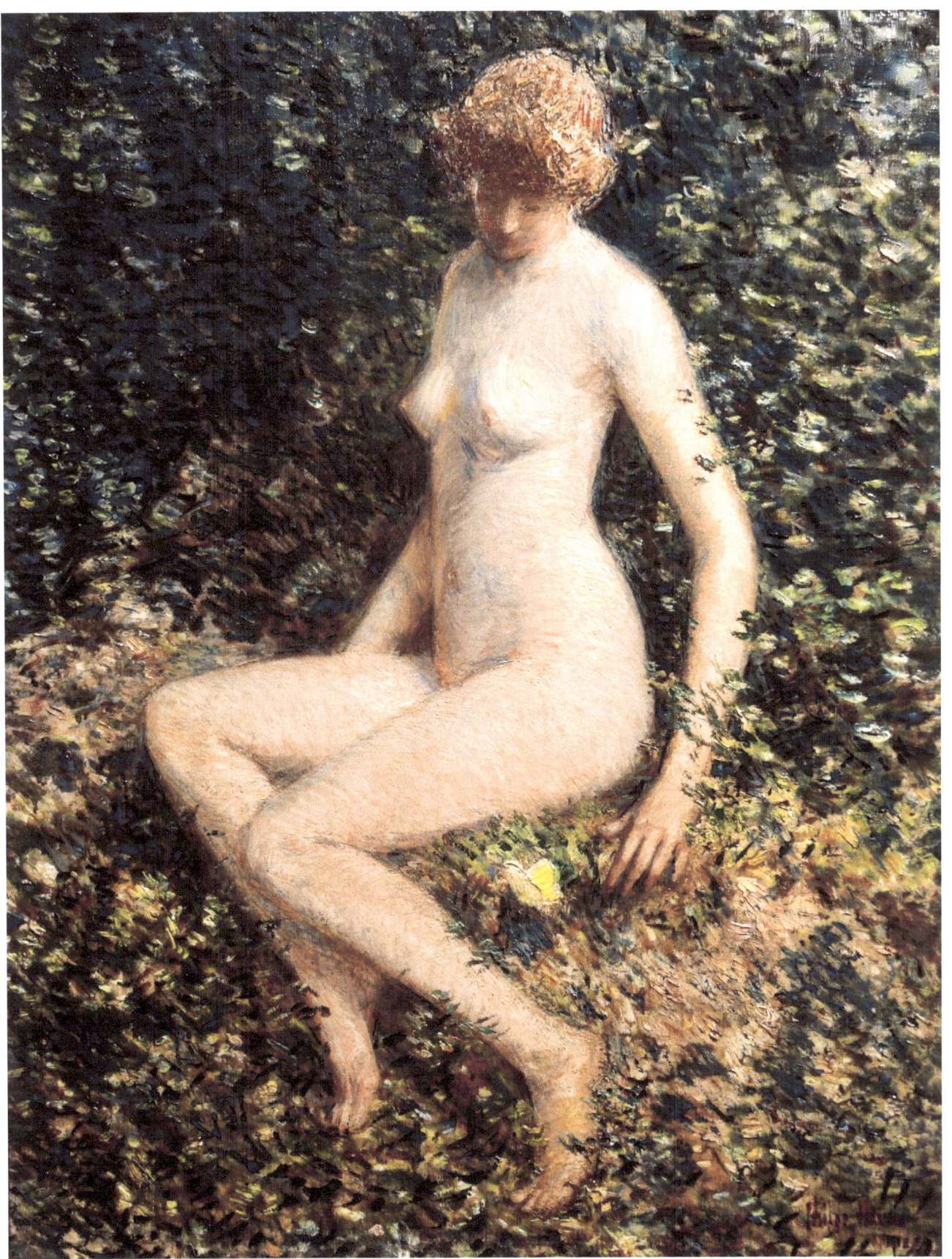

## The Birth of Venus by William Adolphe Bouguereau

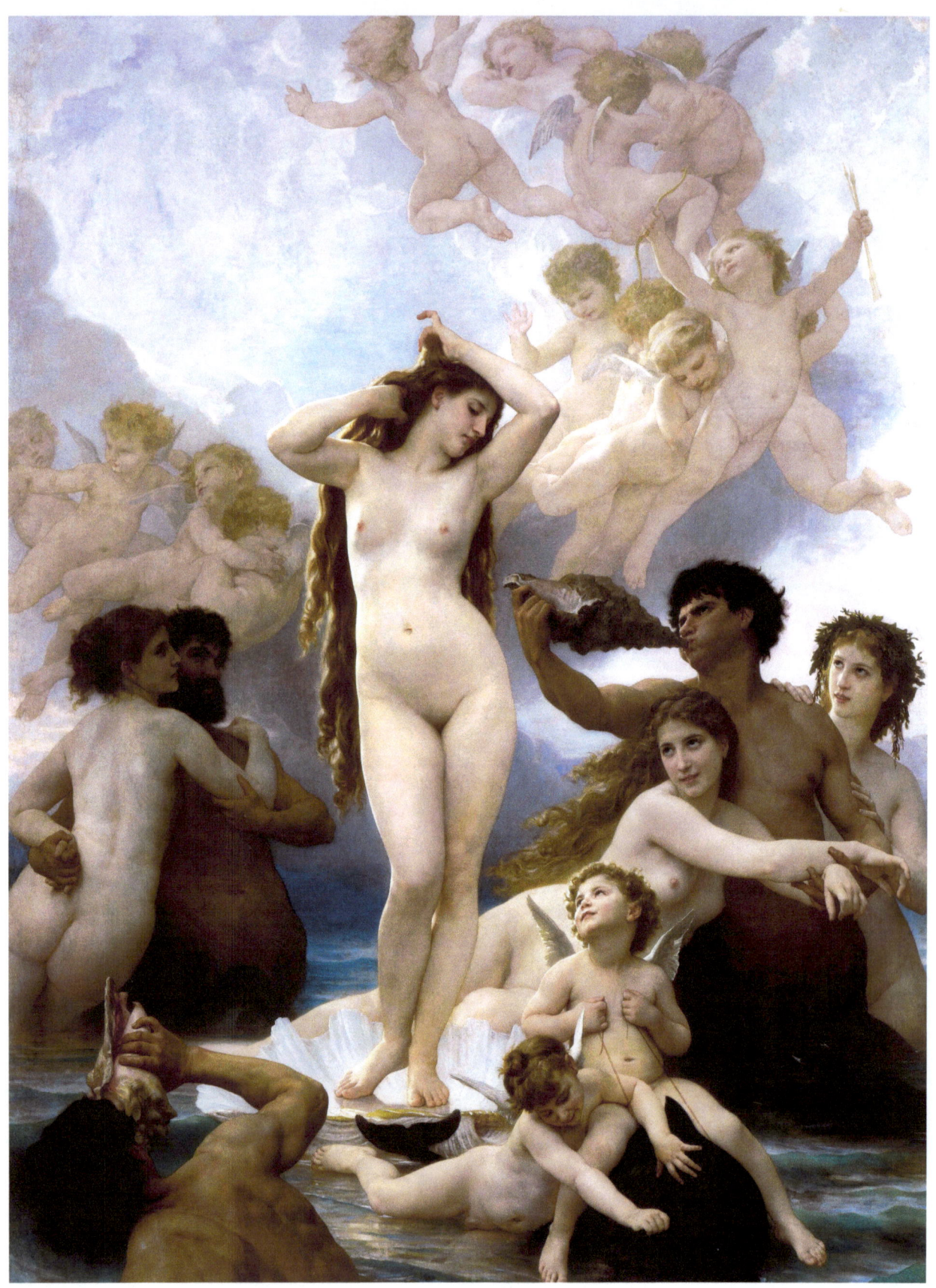

## Le Kimono Japonais by Delphin Enjolras

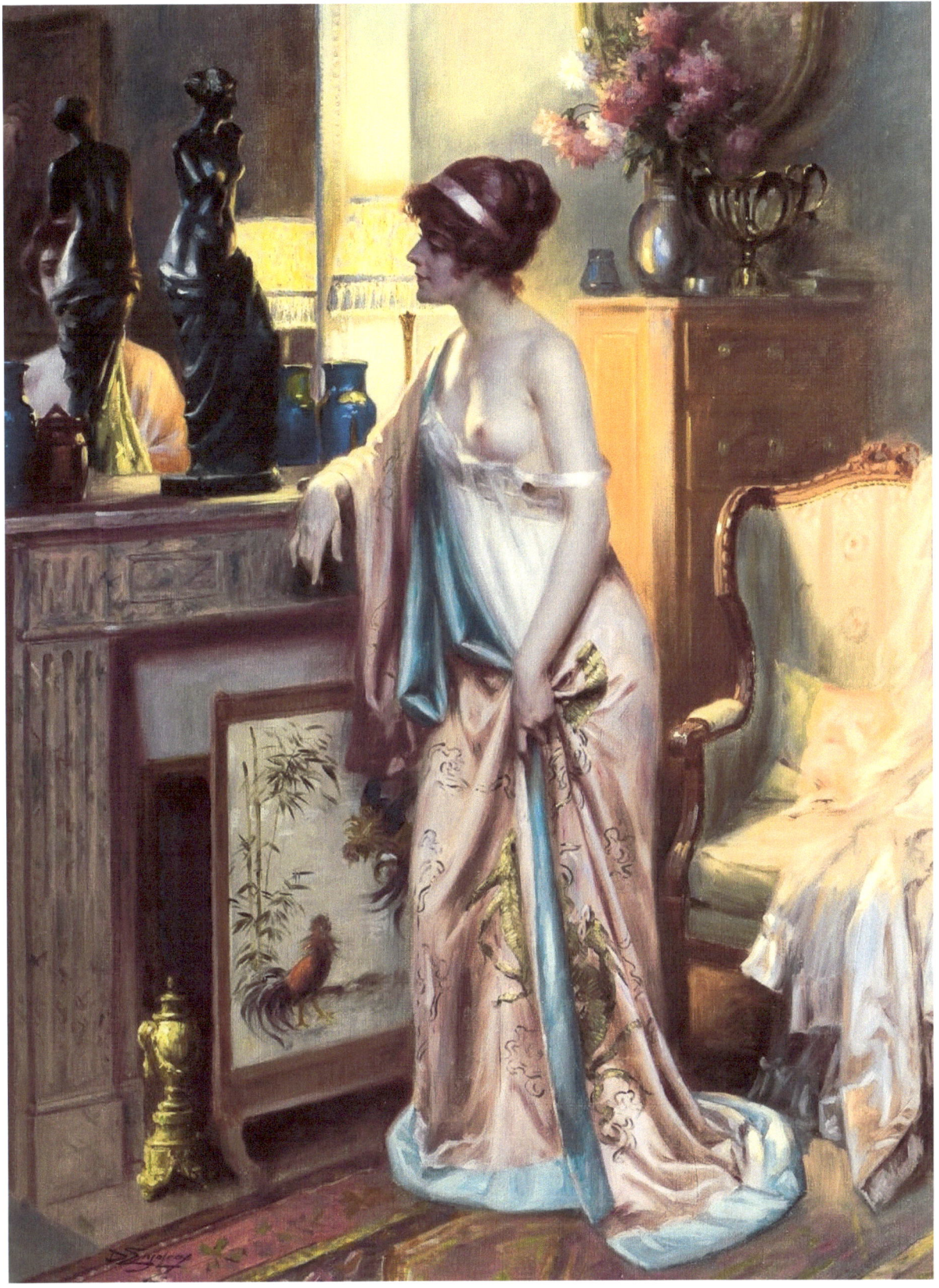

## Cupid & Psyche by William Adolphe Bouguereau

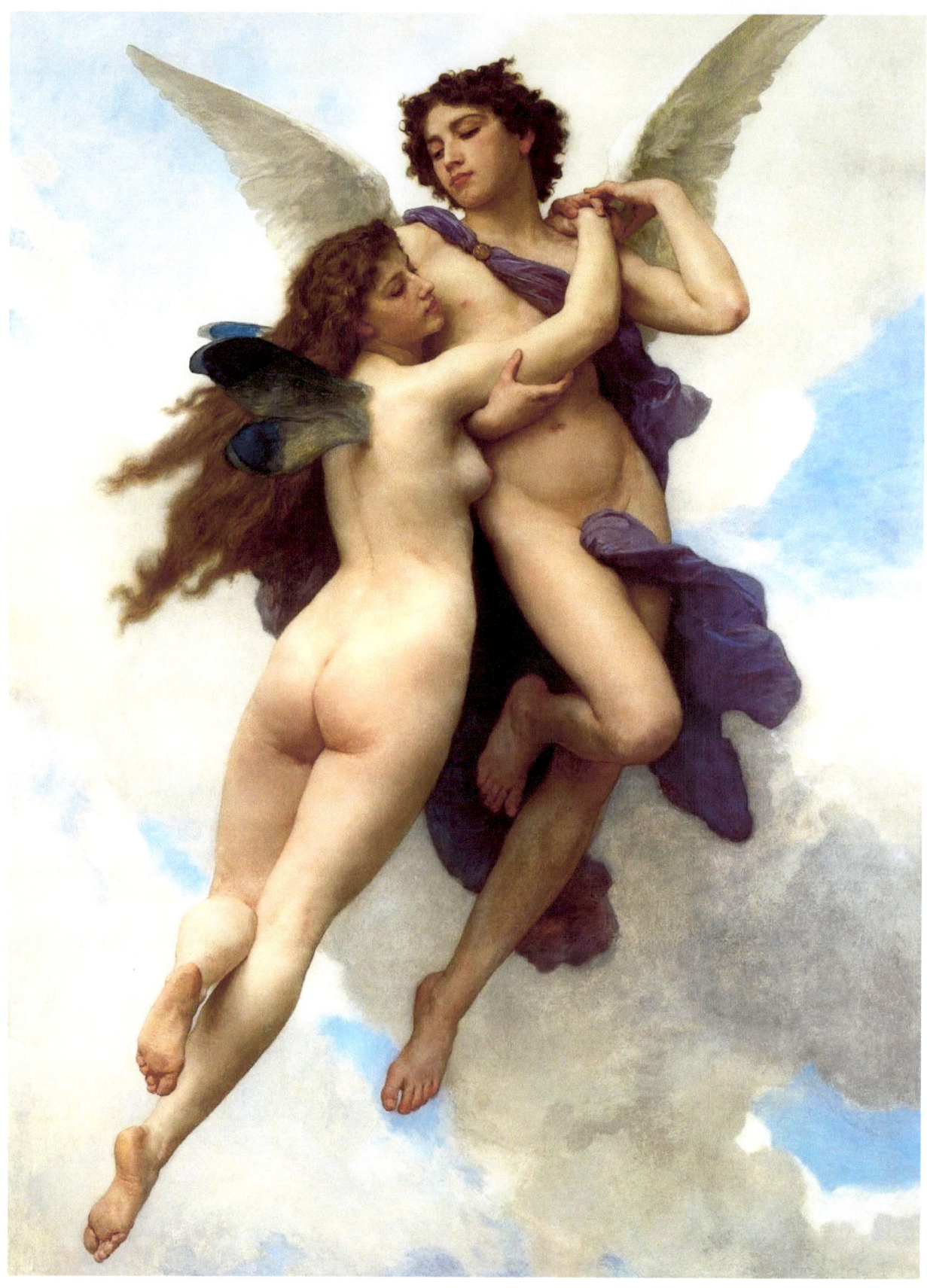

# Venus Verticordia by Dante Gabriel Rossetti

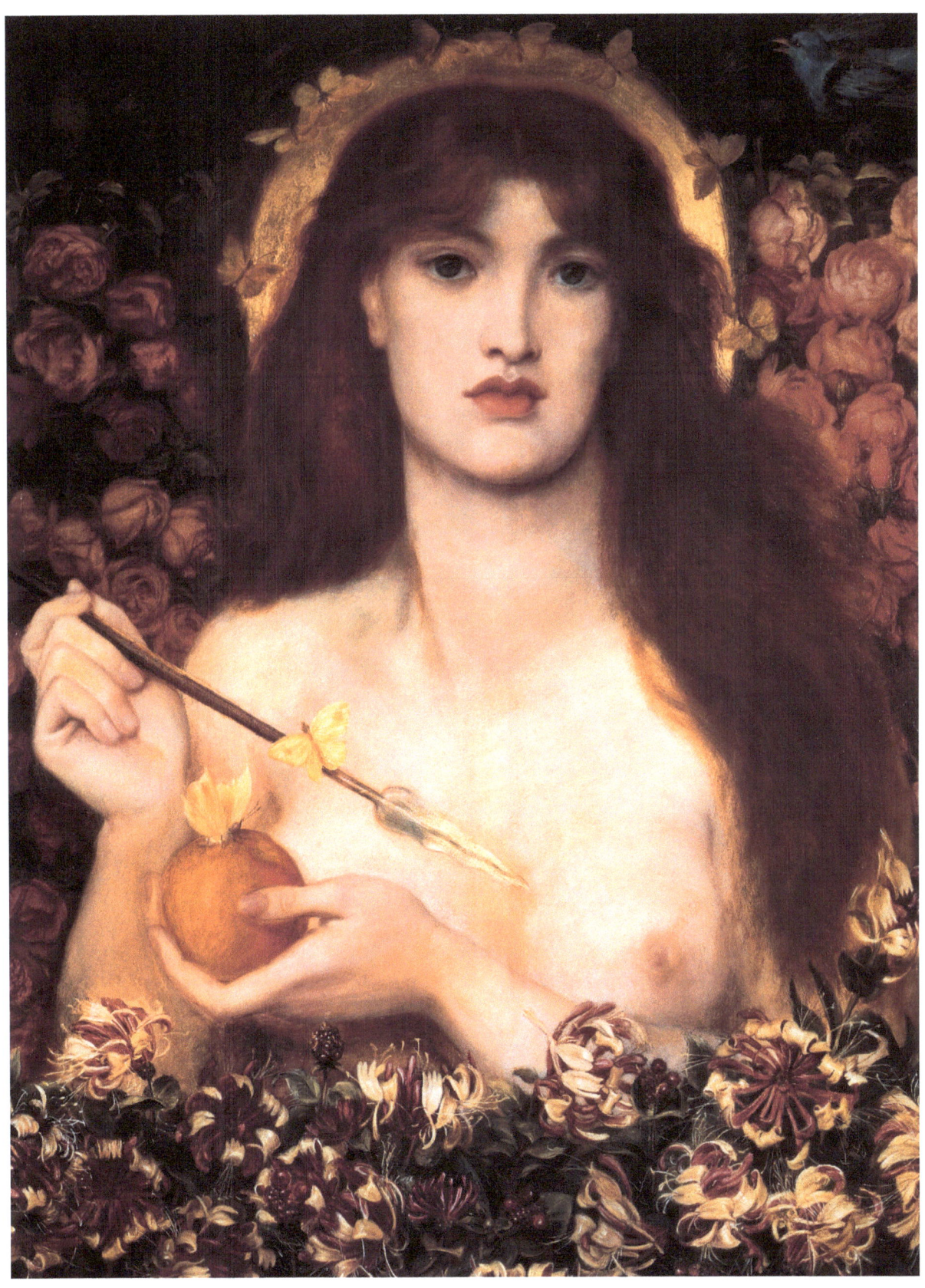

## Chinese Nude at Bath by Qui Ying

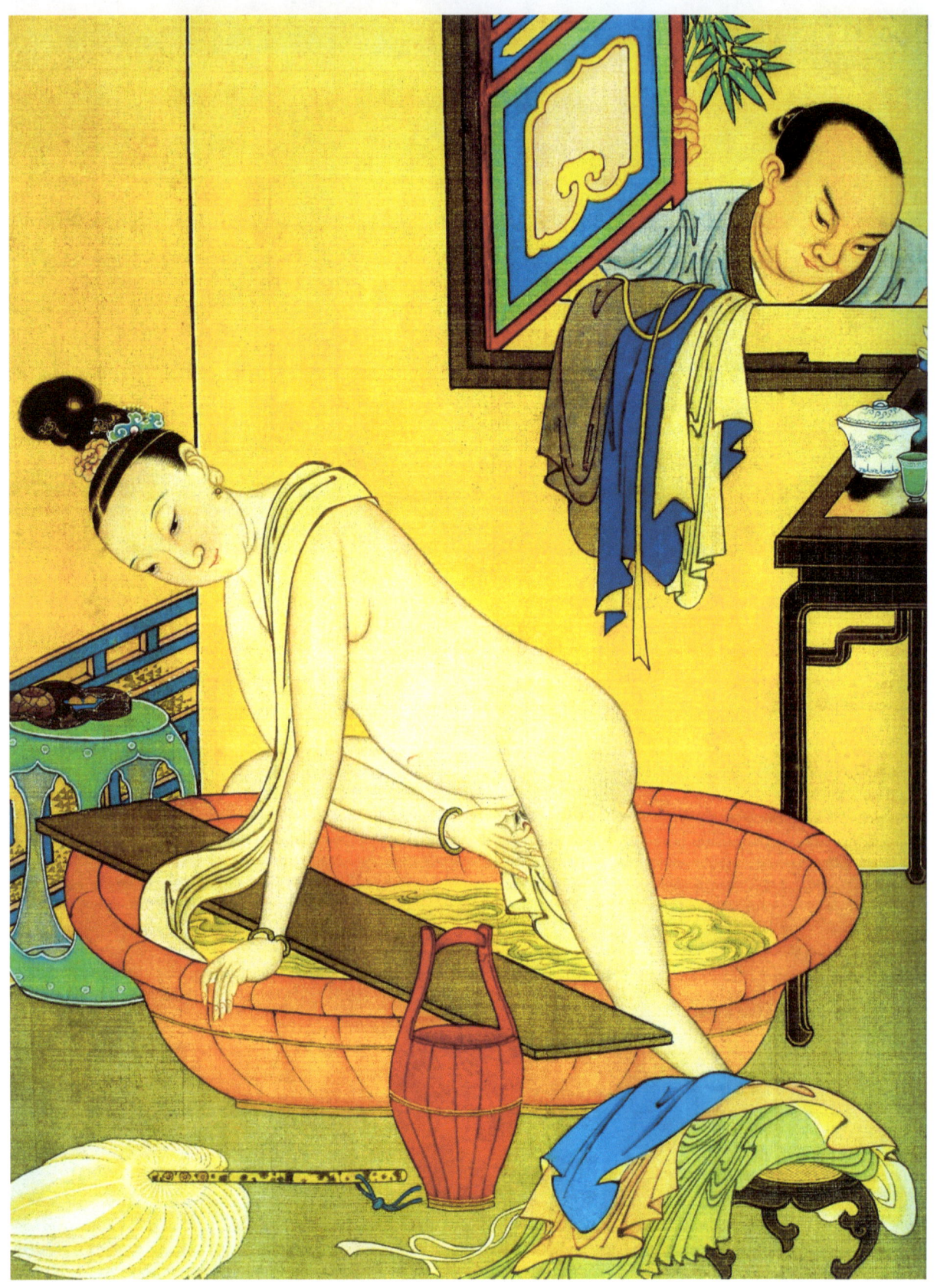

## Eve in the Garden by Paul Ranson

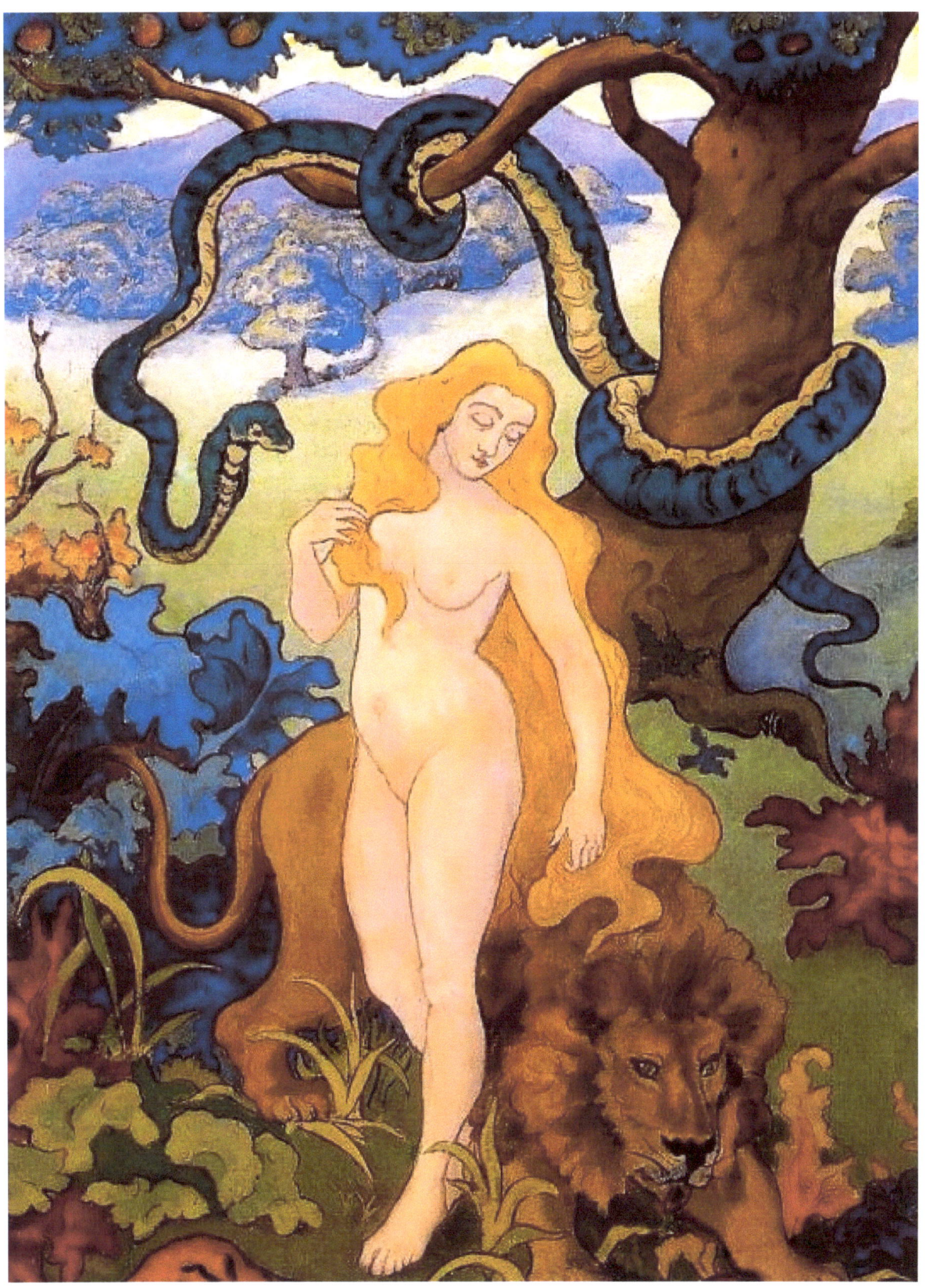

# Adam and Eve by Albrecht Durer

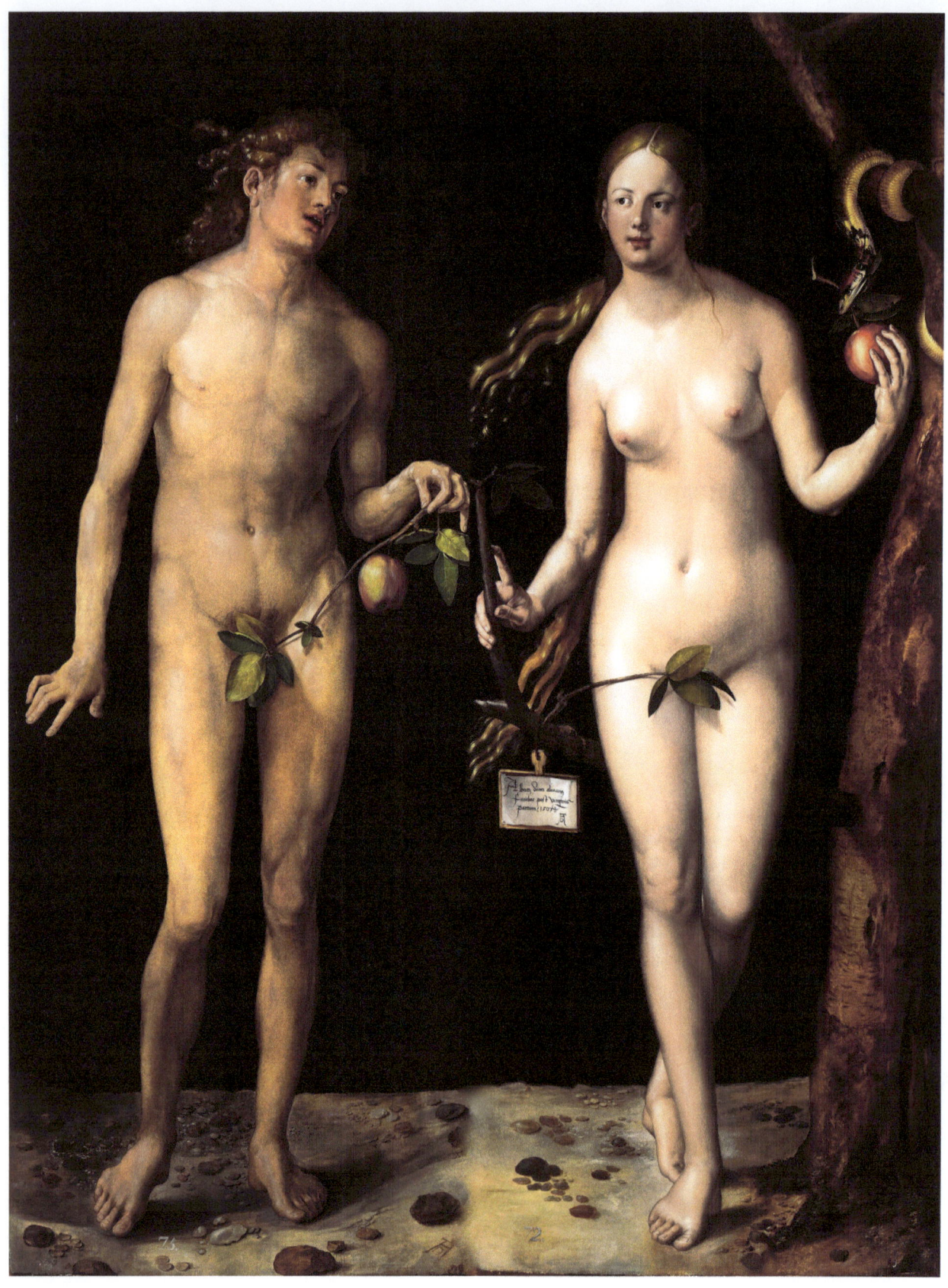

## Nude Bather by Pierre Auguste Renoir

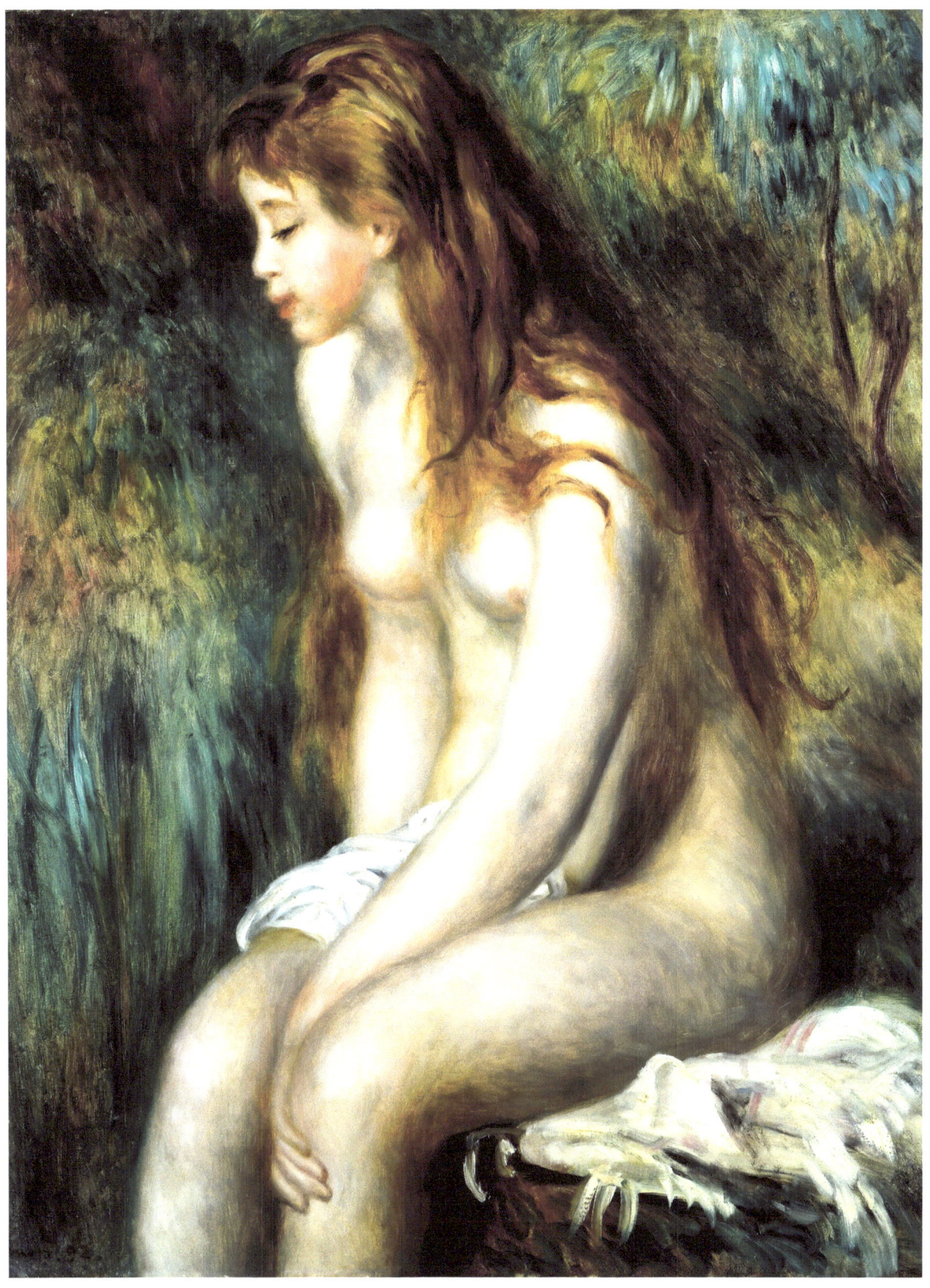

# The Large Bathers by Pierre Auguste Renoir

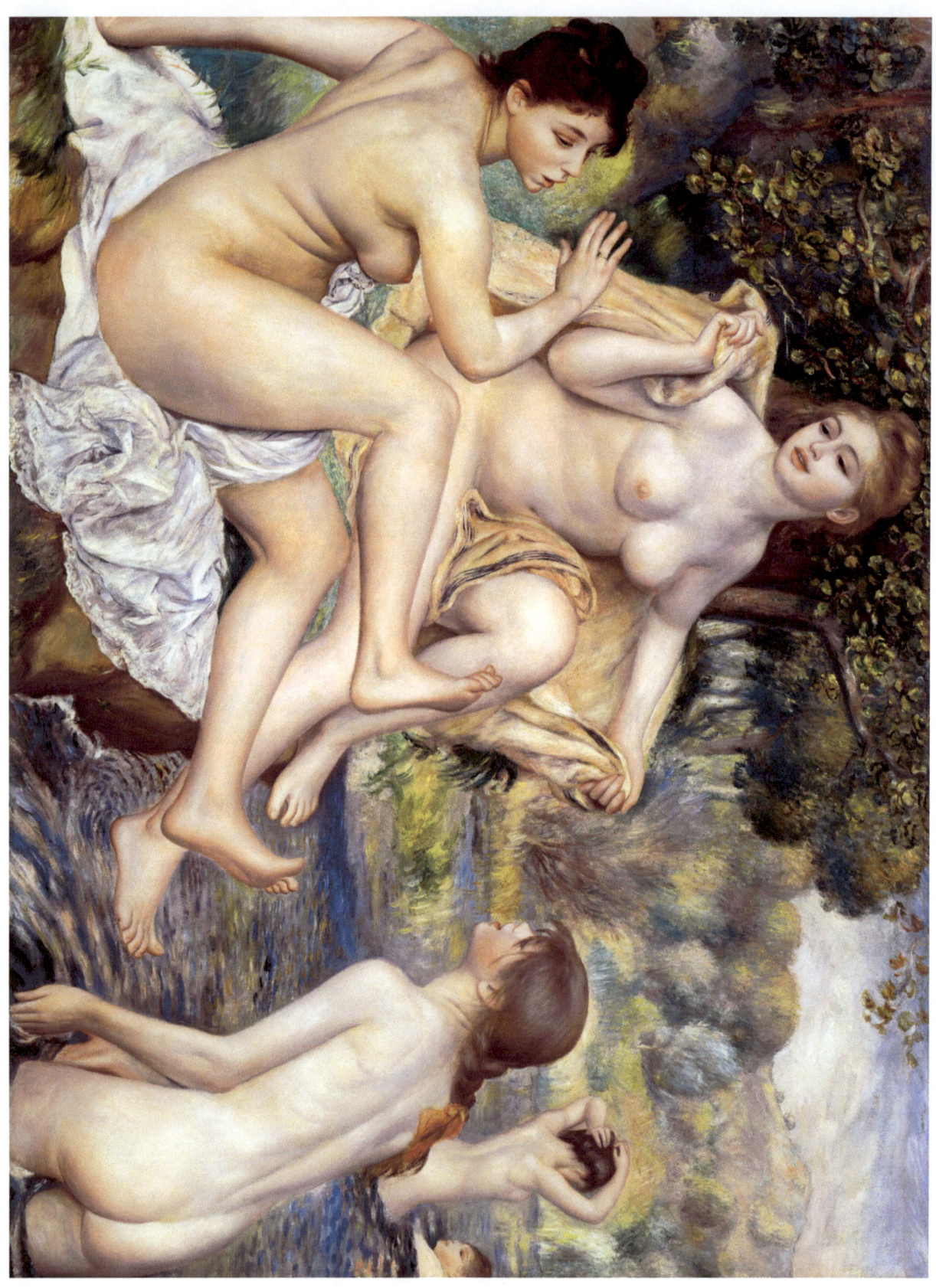

# She Goes Down to the Fresh Water by Paul Gauguin

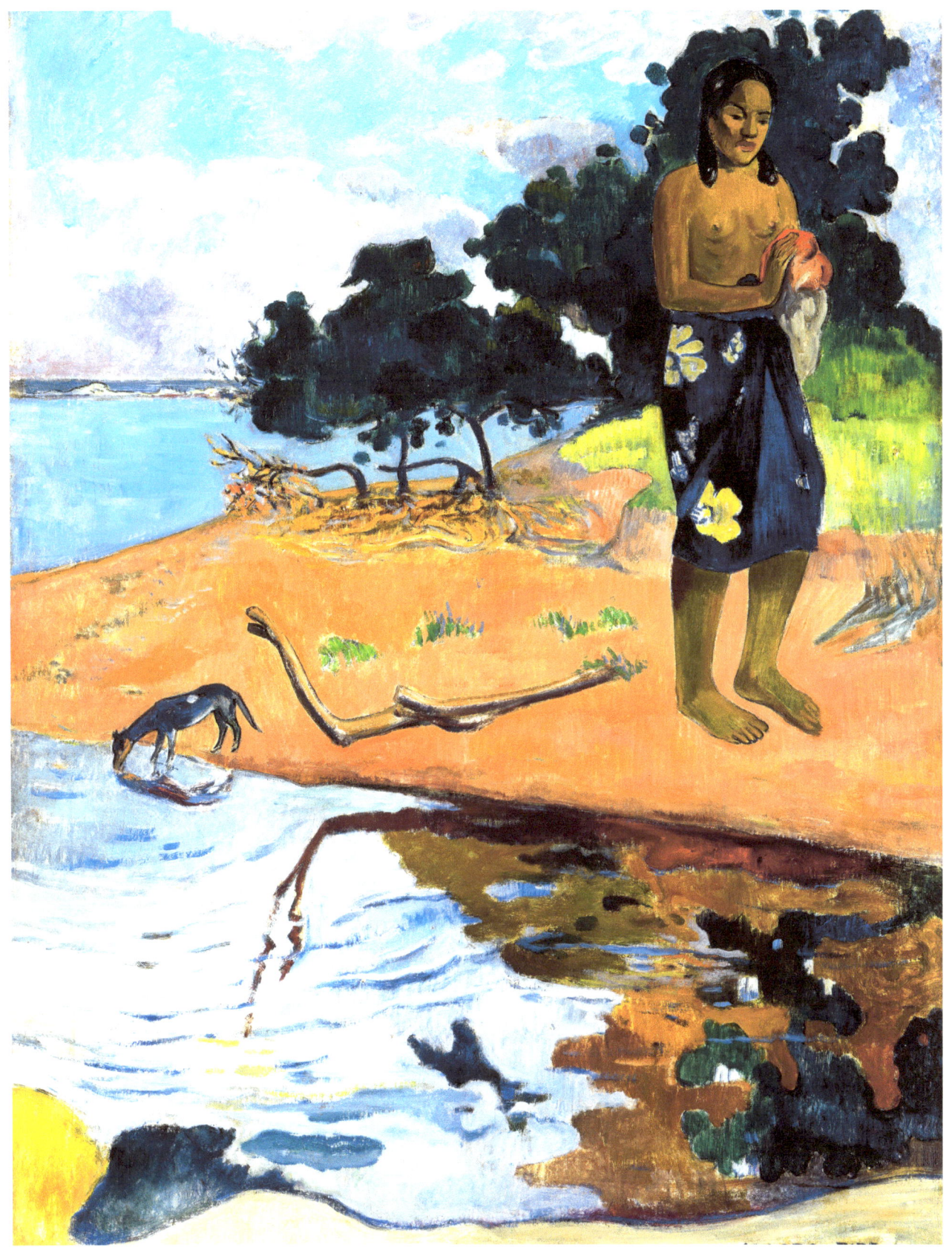

# Nude with a Hat by Vladimir Baranov Rossine

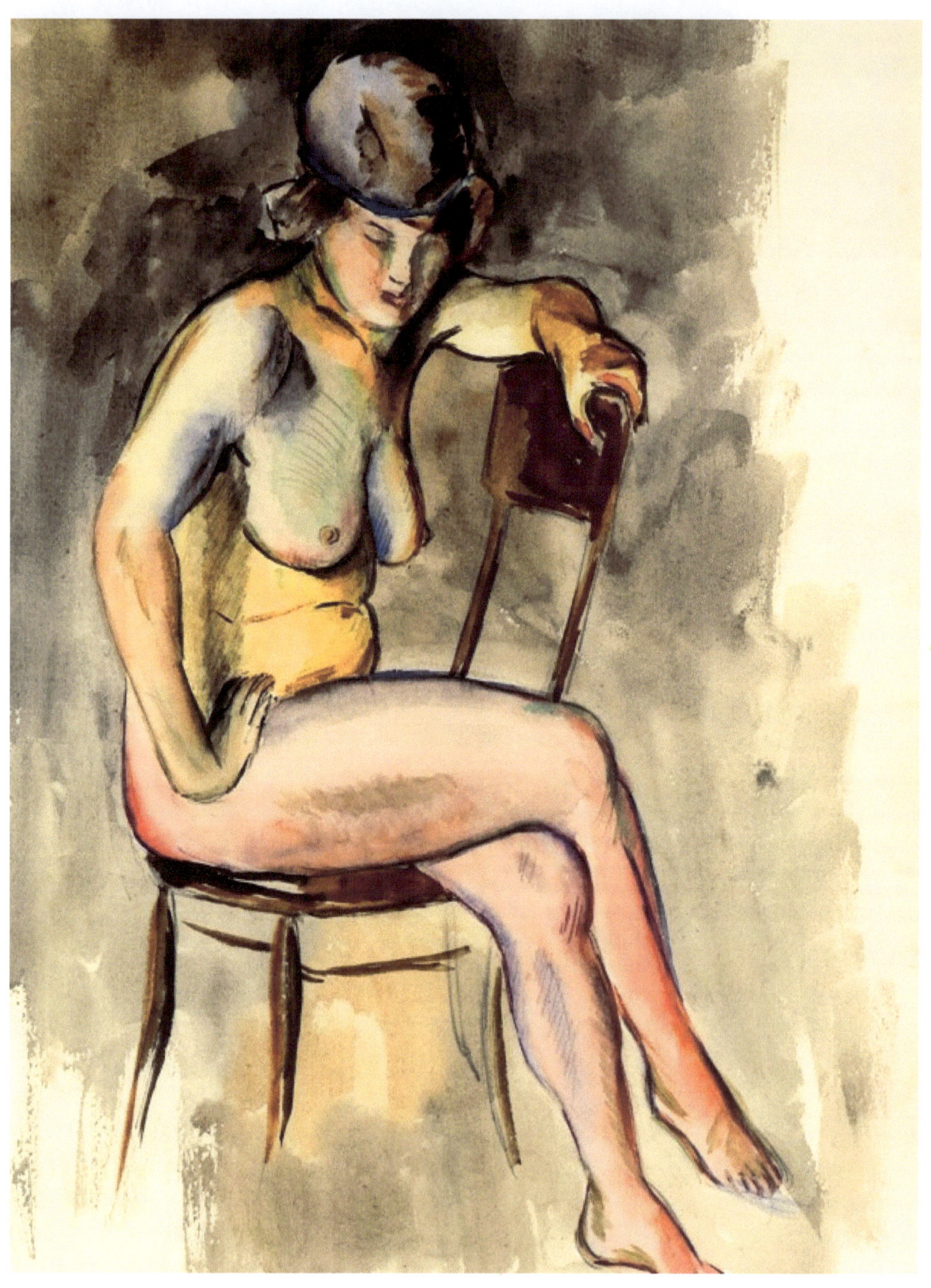

# Nude Sitting by Théo Van Rysselberghe

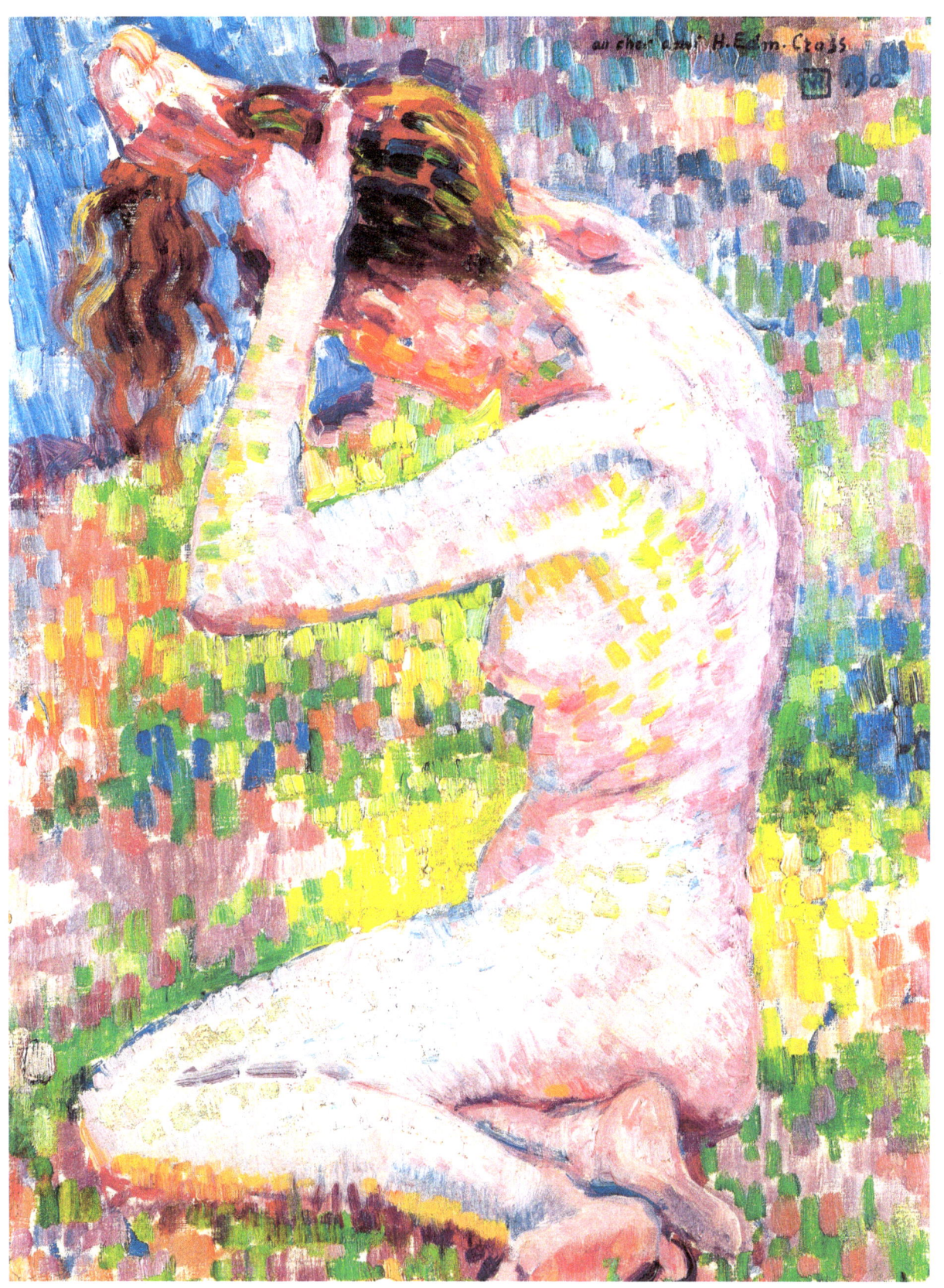

## Reclining Nude by Tsugouharu Foujita

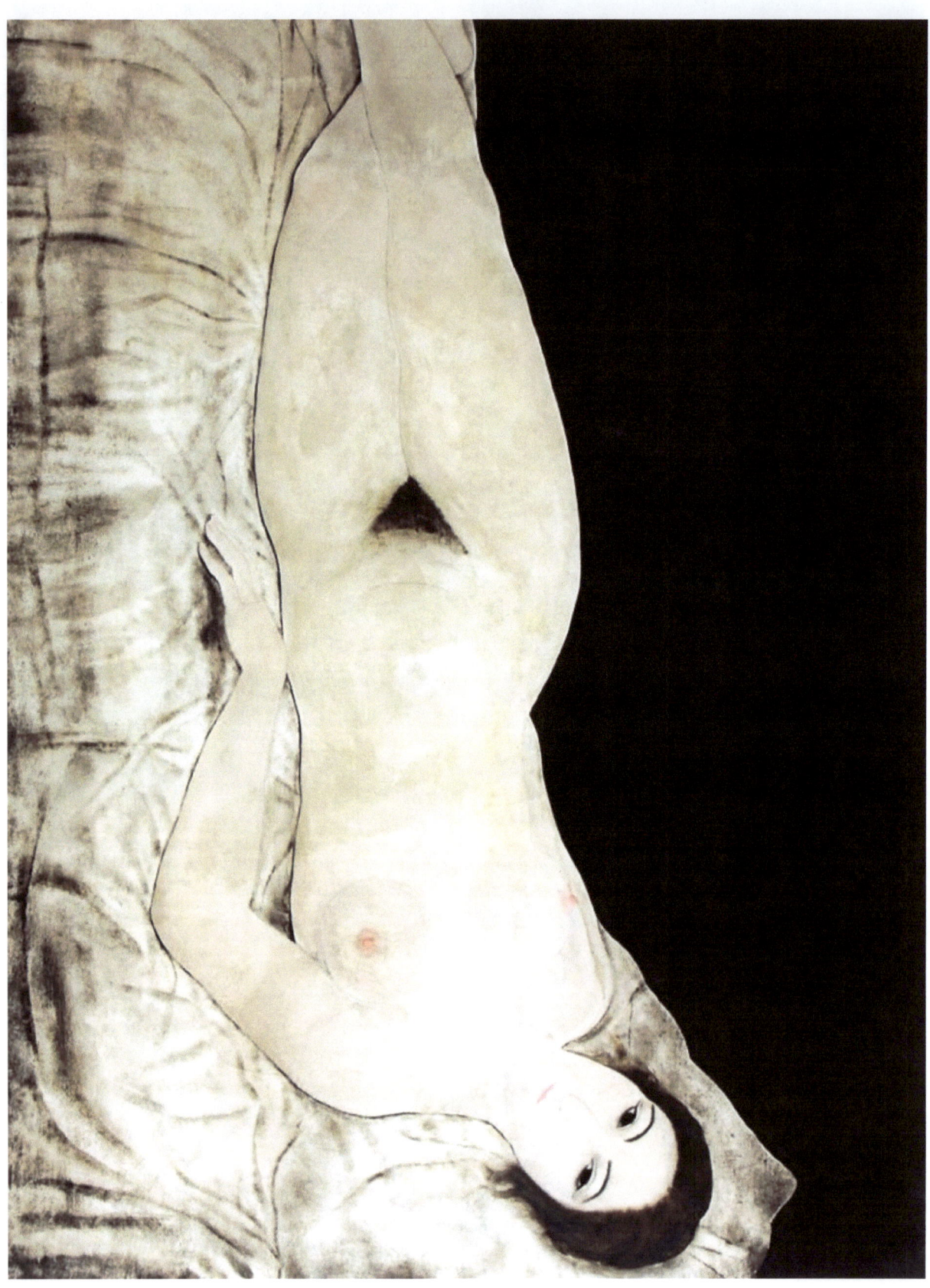

# Nude in Sunlit Wood by Childe Hassam

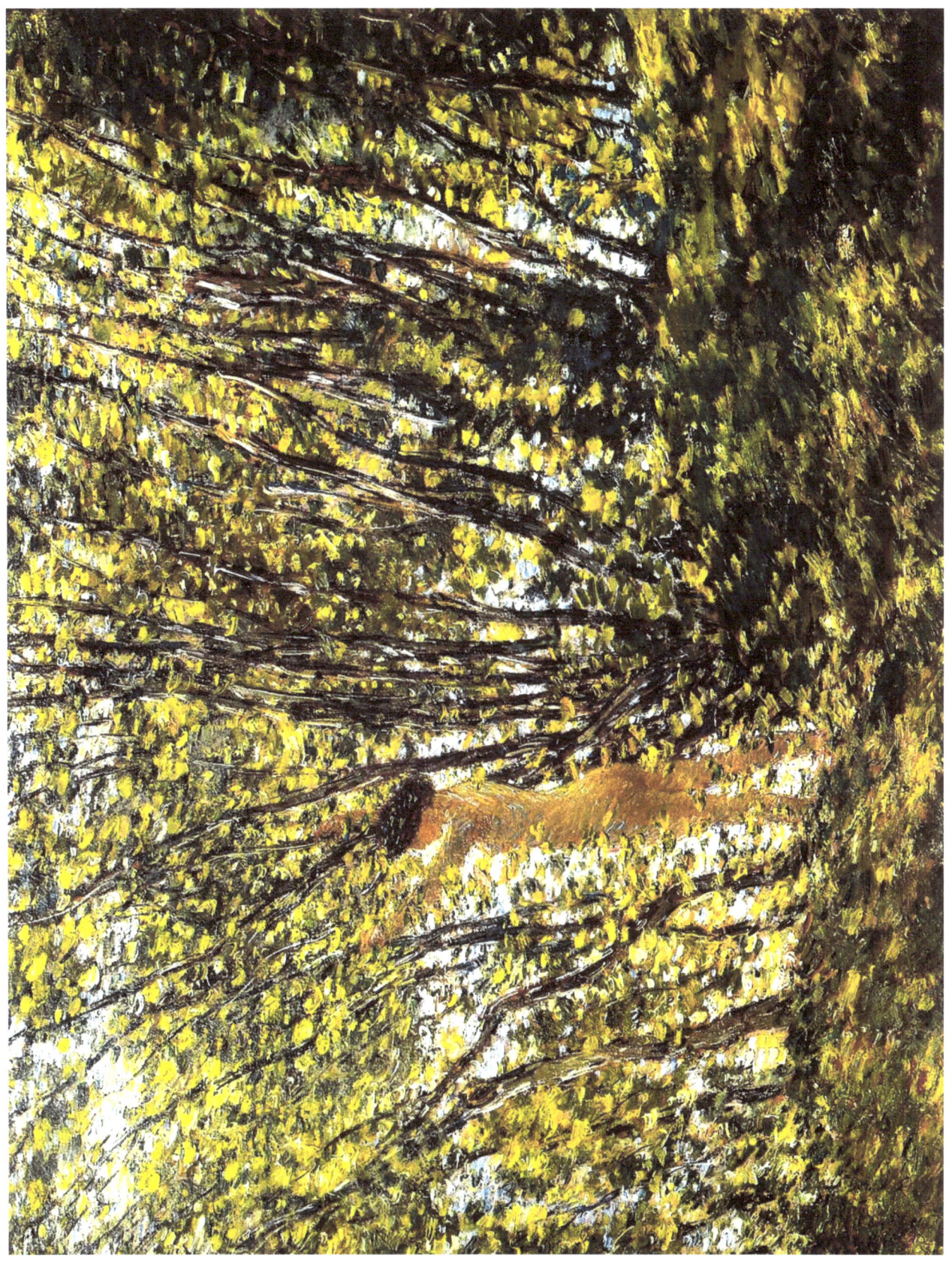

## Woman Lying Down Semi-Nude by Egon Schiele

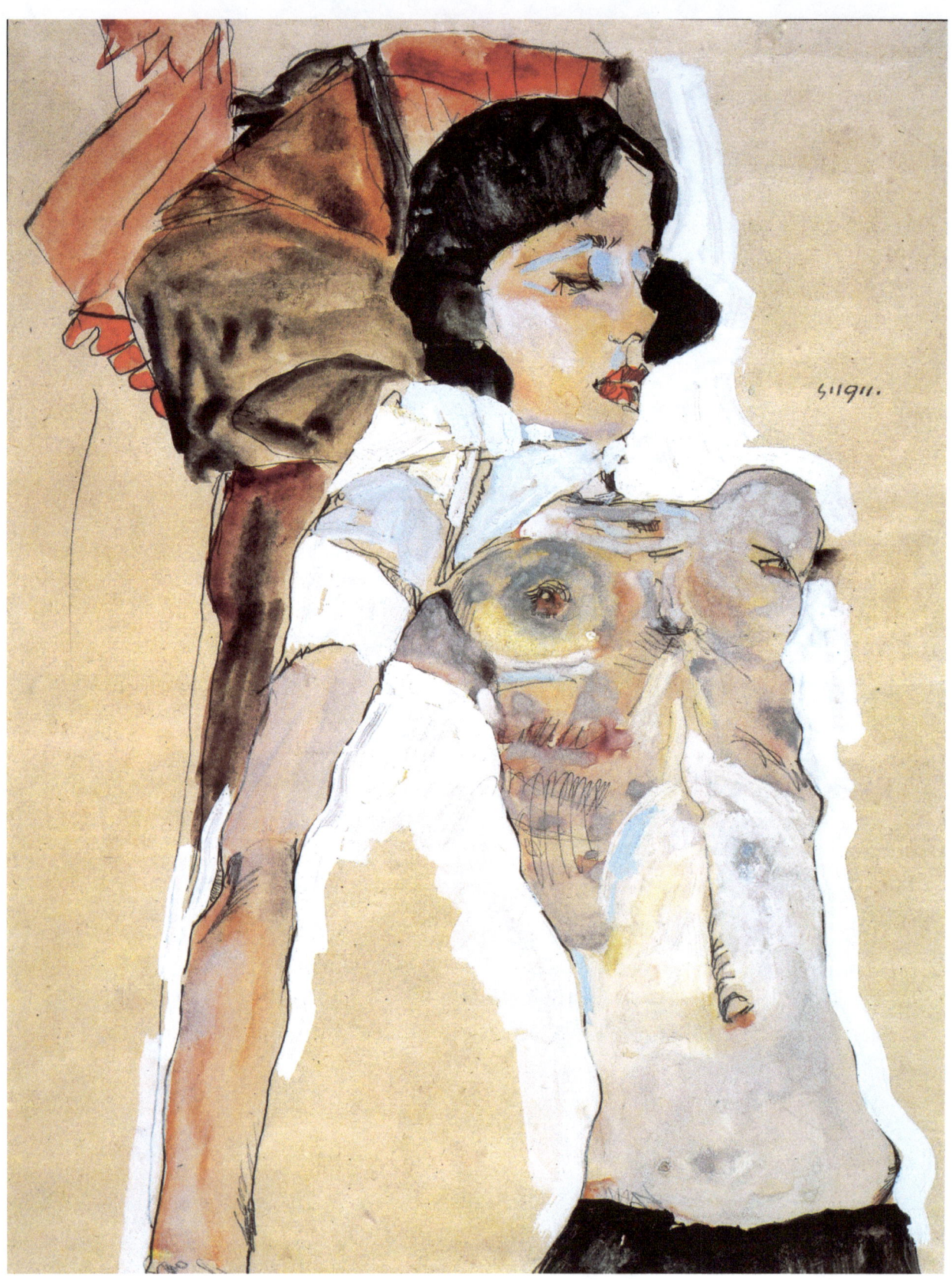

## Dancing Beauty by Hans Zatzka

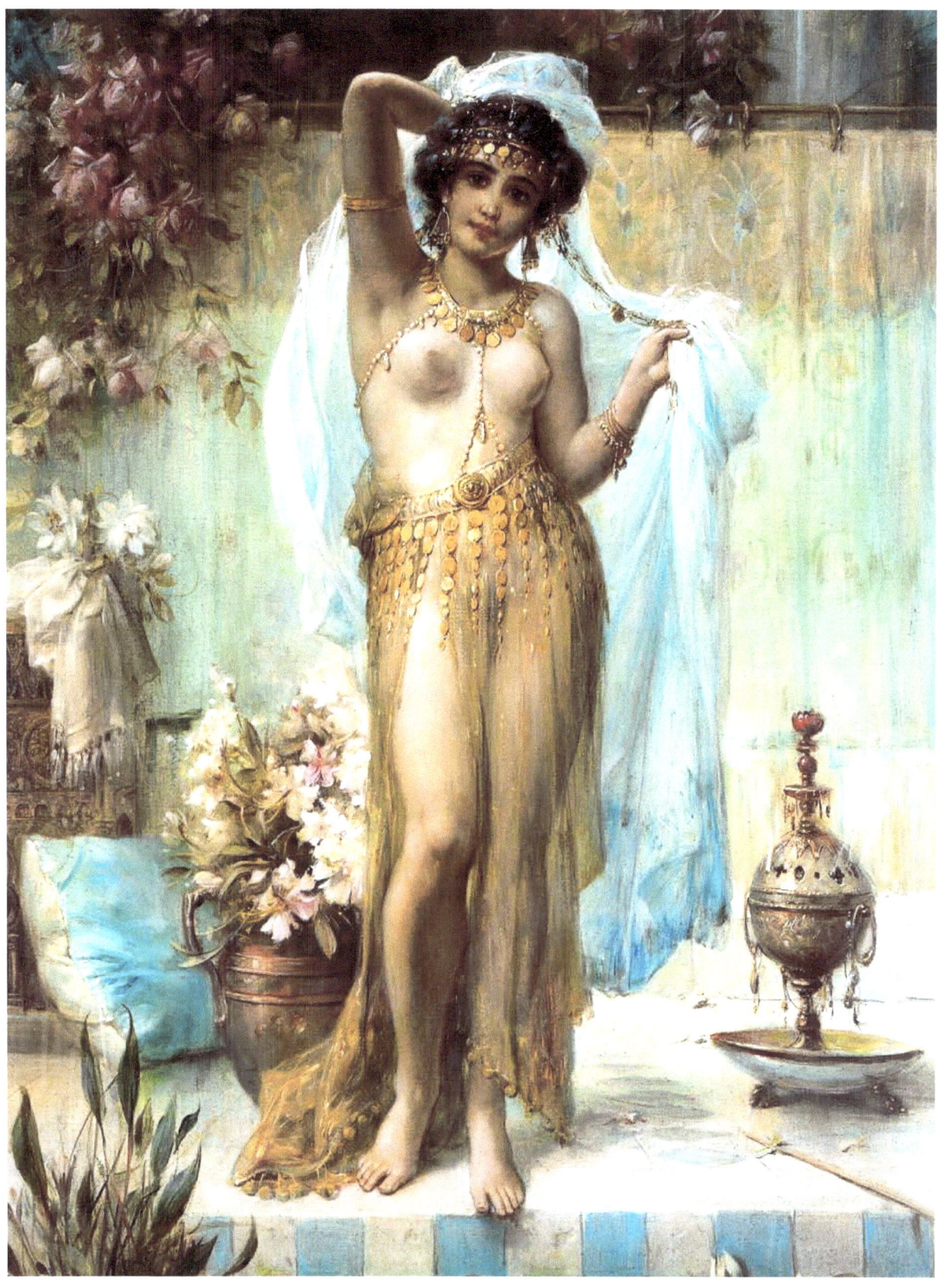

# The Odalisque by Mariano Fortuny

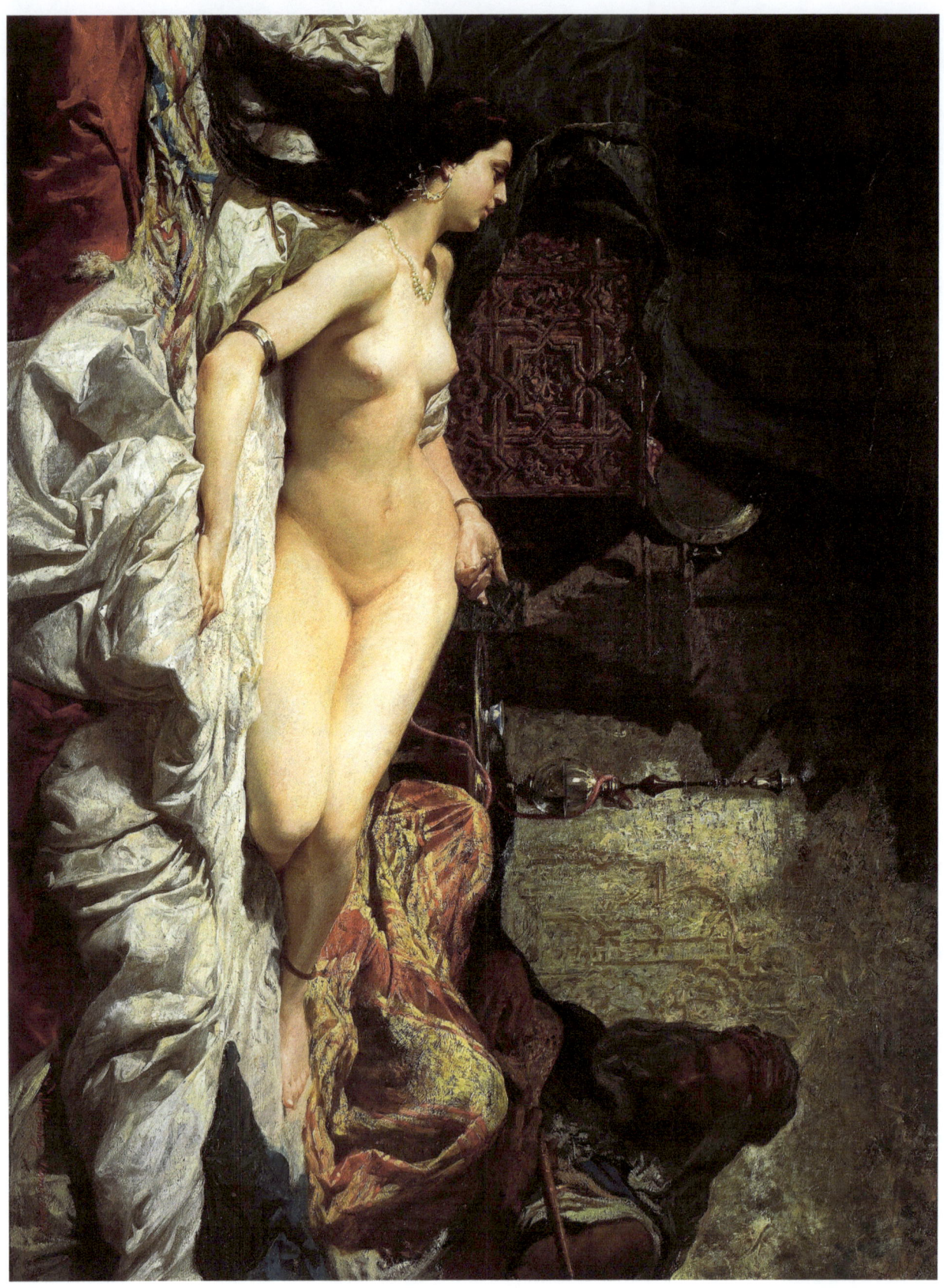

# Study for Female Nude by Nakamura Tsune

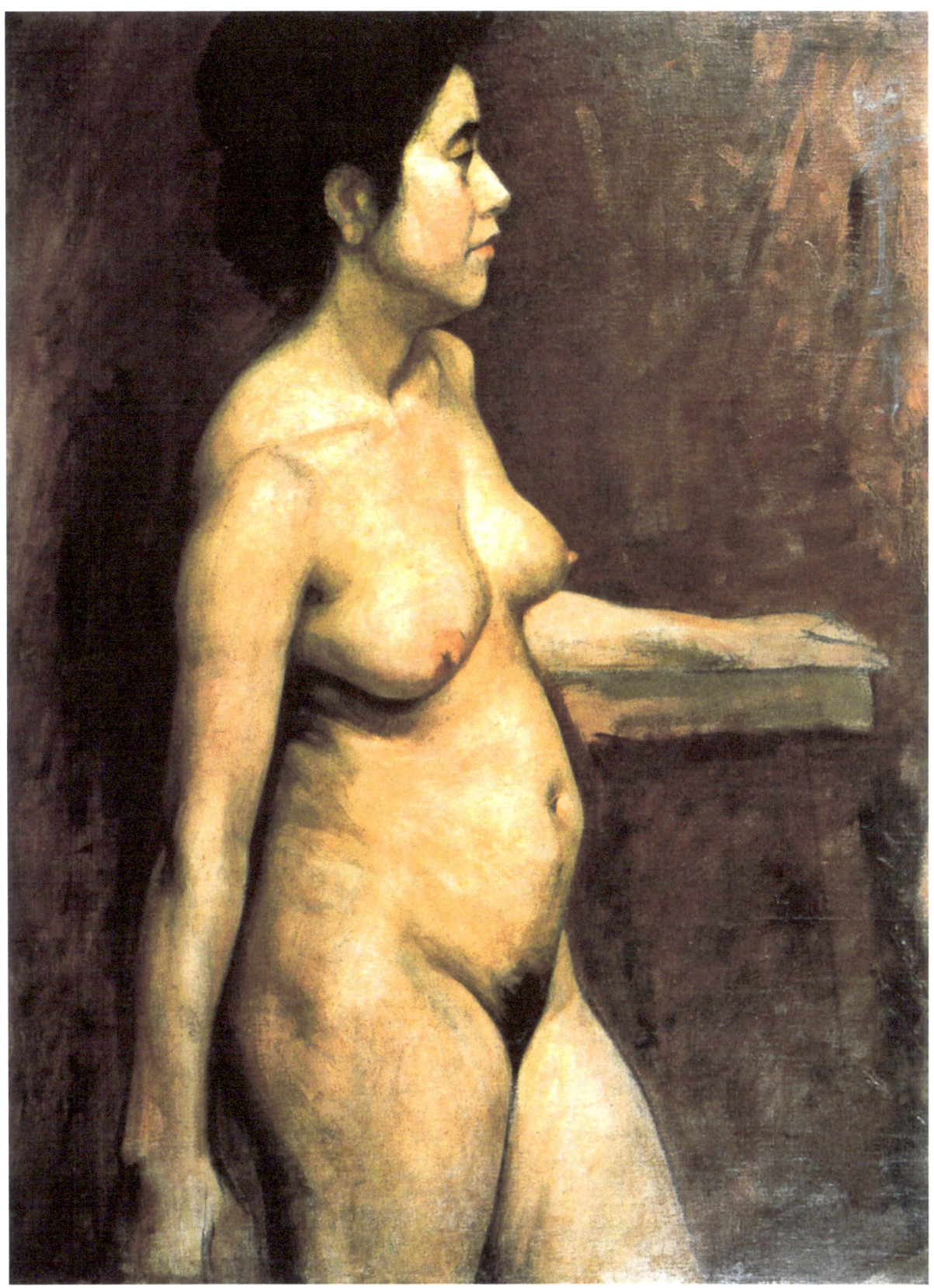

# Oriental Nude by Hans Hassenteufel

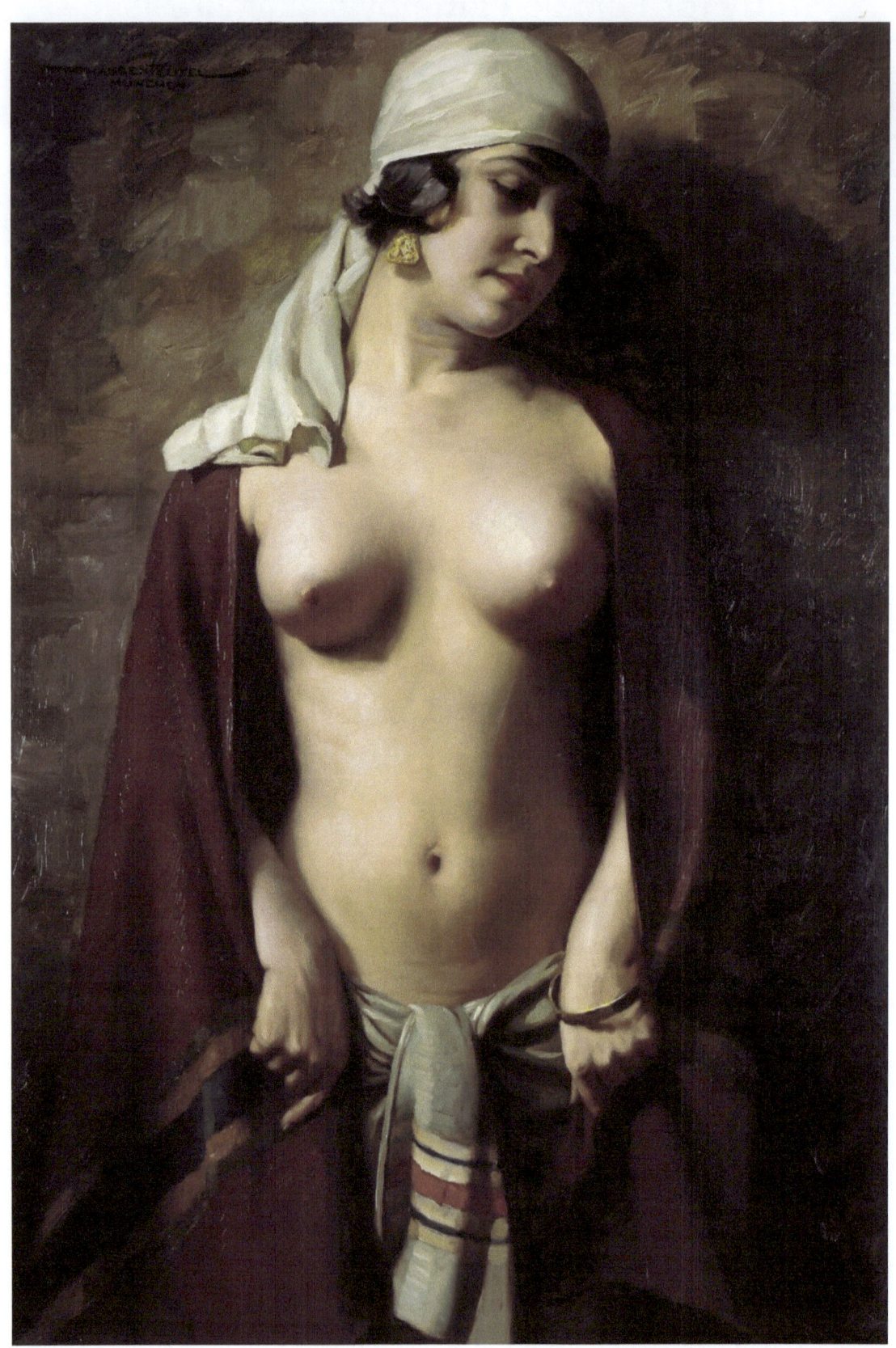

# Without Ceres and Bacchus, Venus Would Freeze by Hendrick Goltzius

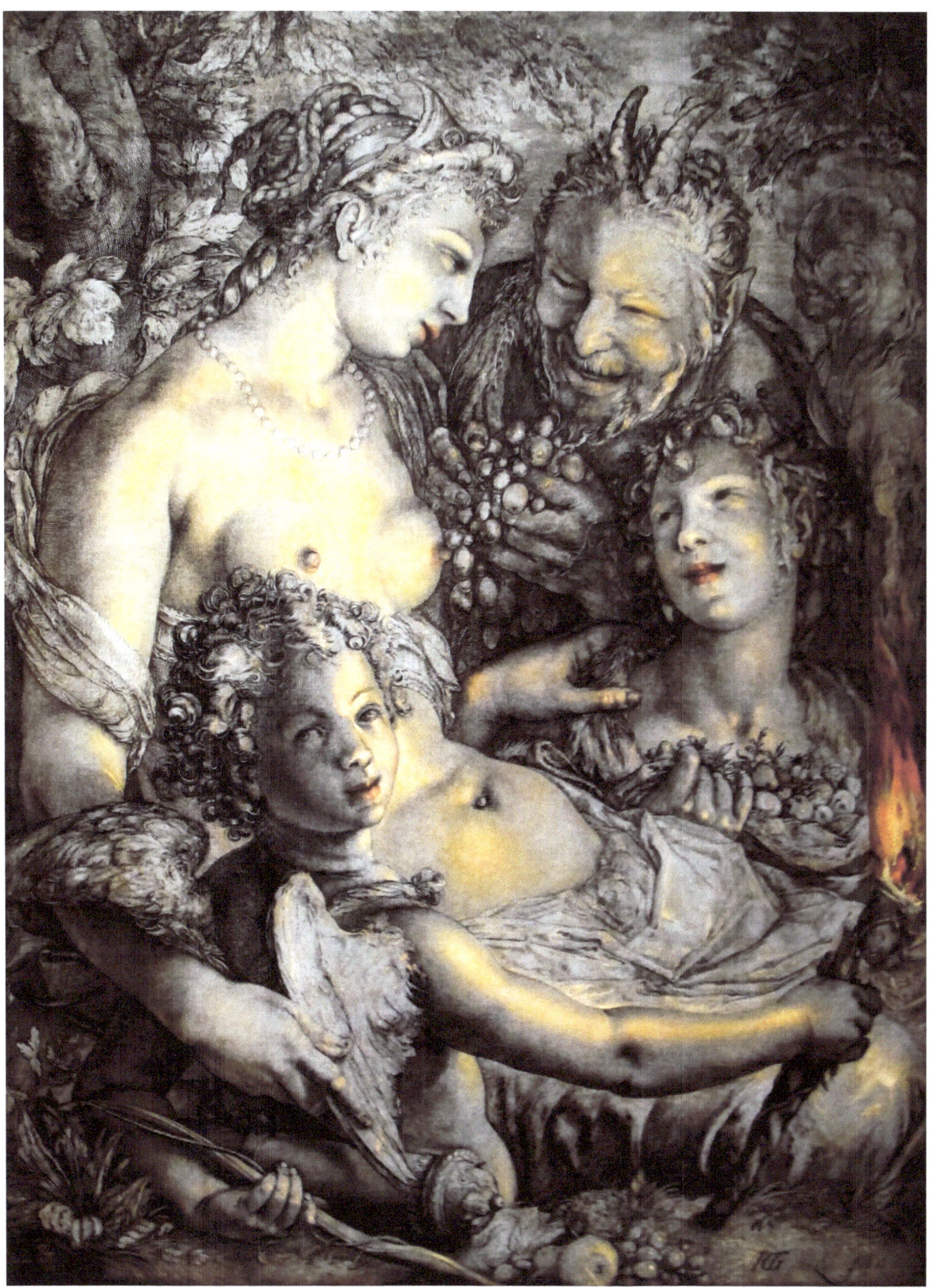

# Nude From Behind by Paul Gauguin

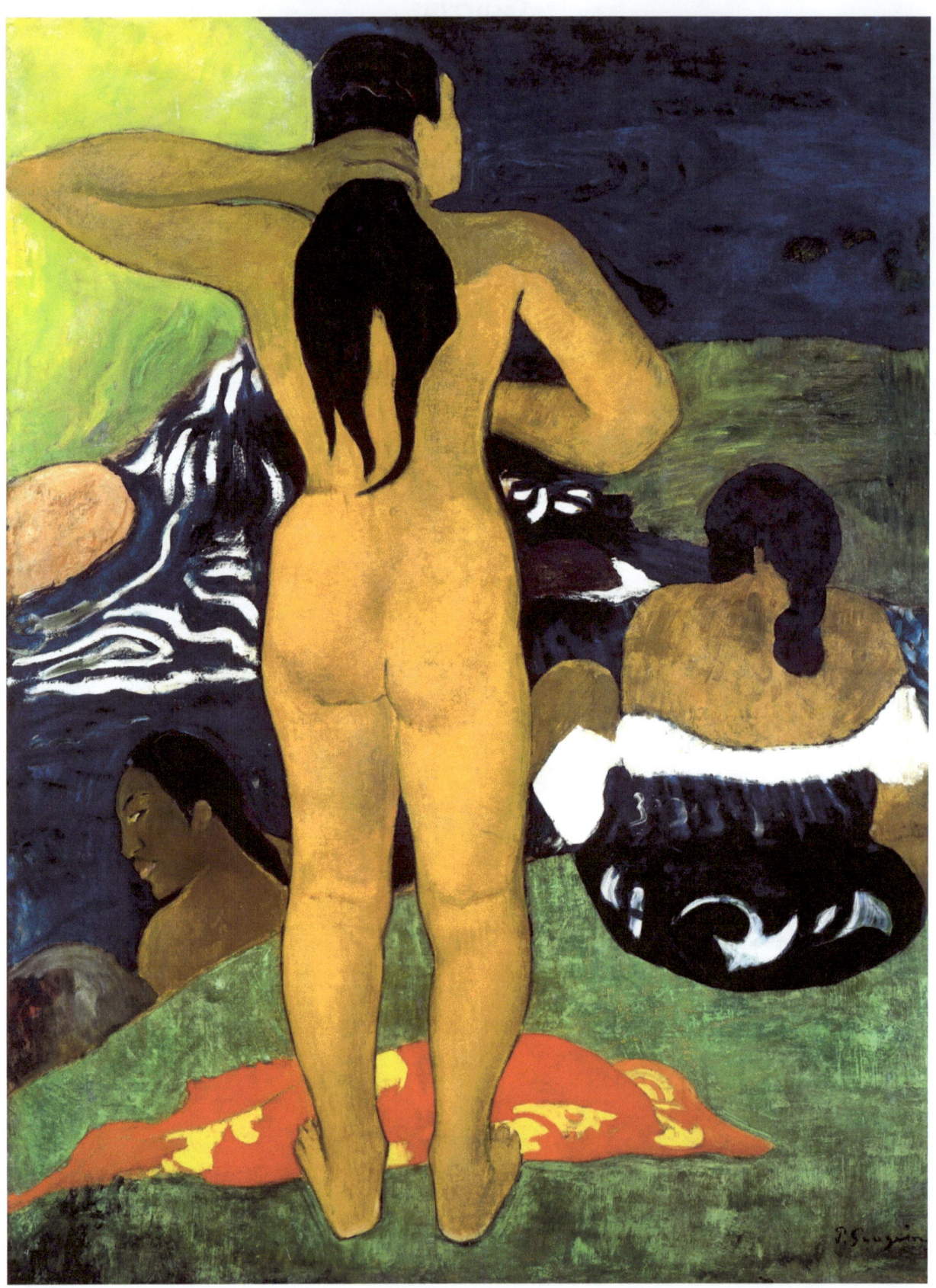

Page 53

# Nude Young Woman Dressing by CW Eckersberg

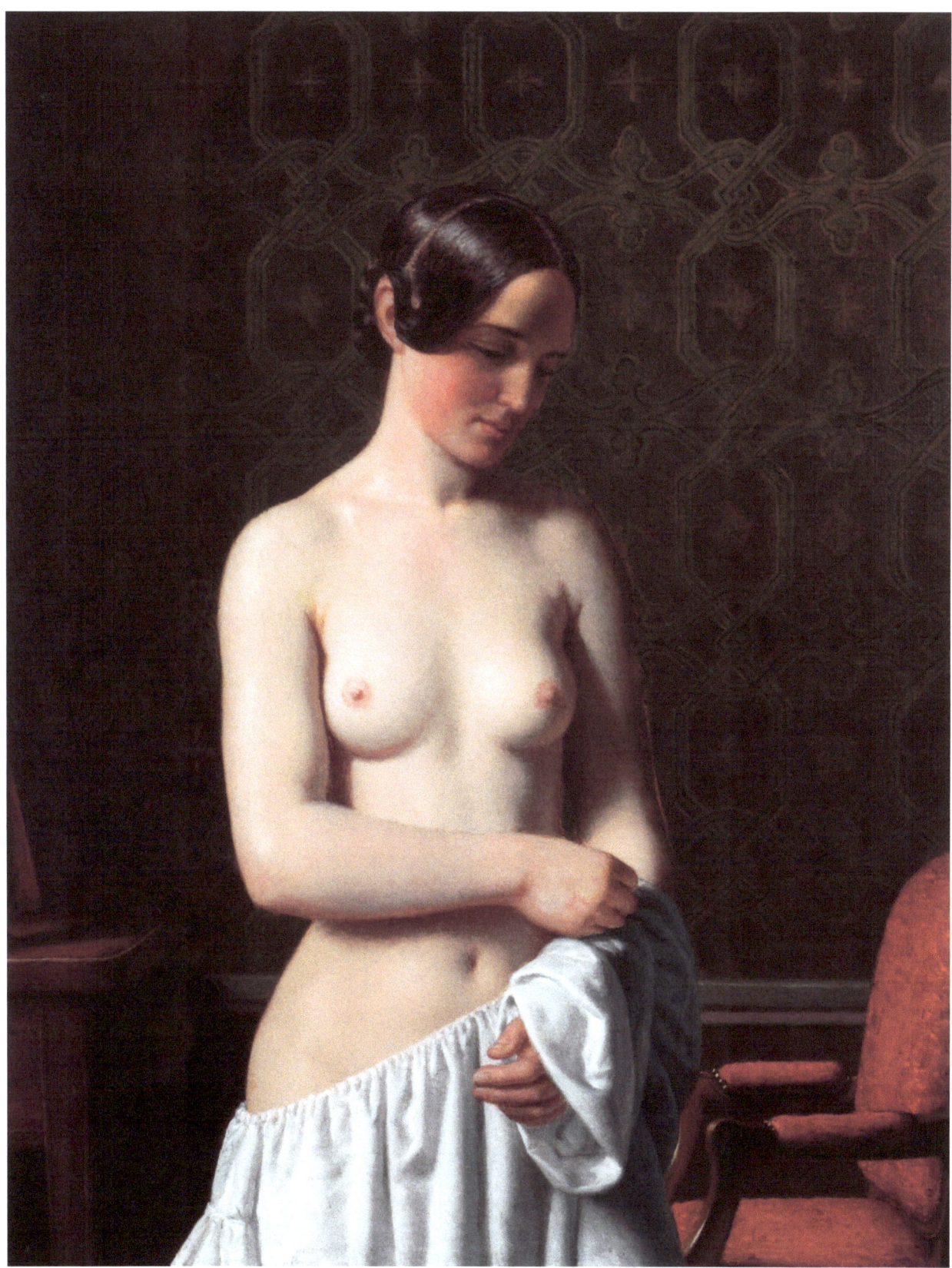

# Sitting Nude With Pillow by August Macke

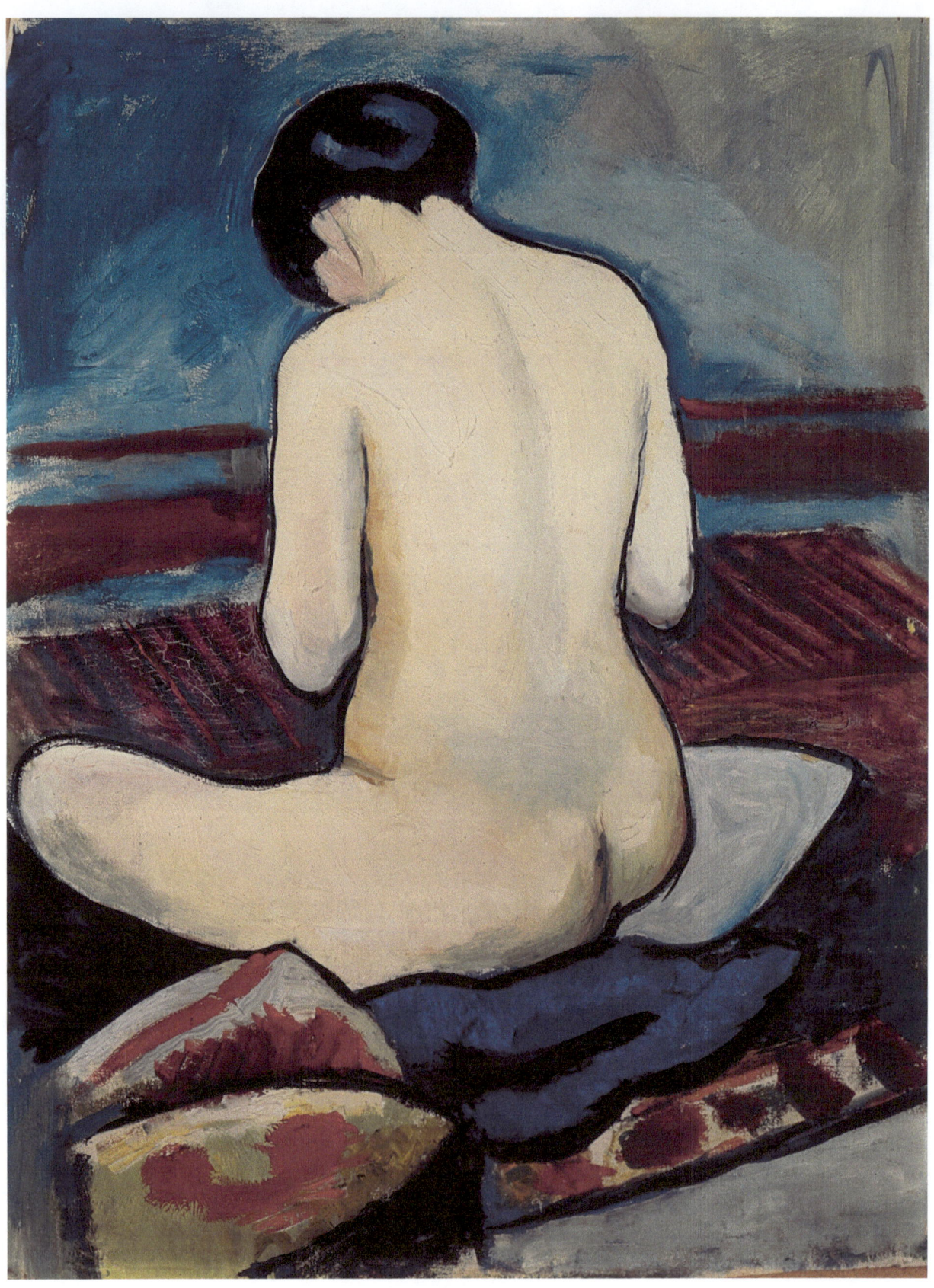

## About The Author

The author of this work currently resides in a small coastal town in Southern Oregon. He owns a small photography publishing business and continues to work on new pictorial books as well as write poetry, stories and other non-fiction works.

## Other Books by the Author on Amazon

**"Classic Fine Art Nudes: Volume One."** This book is the previous book in my series on classic fine art nudes and is available on Amazon at https://www.amazon.com/Classic-Fine-Art-Nudes-One/dp/1093912073.

**"Vintage Nudes of Yesteryear"** which features sixty-five black and white photos of nude women produced generally between the years 1900 and 1923. It can be found on Amazon here: https://www.amazon.com/Vintage-Nudes-Yesteryear-Scott-Harker/dp/107044023X.

**"Am I Indigenous and Other Poems"** which can be found on Amazon here: https://www.amazon.com/Am-I-Indigenous-Other-Poems/dp/1689862424. – A collection of poems written between late 2016 and Autumn 2019.

**"Poems By My Cat"** – This book collects a cycle of cat poems which show cats' view of the world and can be found on Amazon here: https://www.amazon.com/Poems-Cat-Carl-Scott-Harker/dp/1793903239.

**"100 Classic Poems to Read at Christmas Time"** which can be found here: https://www.amazon.com/dp/B07J9YS7QK

**"50 Great Poems to Read & Perform Out Loud"** which can be found here: https://amzn.to/2zz8GFT

**"Seeds of Poetry: 21 Methods to Inspire Your Poetry and Other Creative Writings"** – a book about writing your own poetry. It is available on Amazon at https://amzn.to/2HtMpO7

**"Exploring The Universe: The Art of Space"** - Through the use of instruments such as the Hubble Space Telescope, scientists have captured the colorful art that space itself creates. Here is the link: https://www.amazon.com/Exploring-Universe-Carl-Scott-Harker-ebook/dp/B077XQRPQL

---

## Copyright Notice

Cover design by Carl Scott Harker

Copyright © 2019 Carl Scott Harker

*Note: The artworks presented in this book are in the public domain. The book, as published, is, of course, copyrighted.*

An Aldouspi Publication

www.ingramcontent.com/pod-product-compliance
Lightning Source LLC
Chambersburg PA
CBHW051214220526
45473CB00003B/1024